Feasting on the Word®

WORSHIP COMPANION

Feasting on the Word®
WORSHIP COMPANION

❧ LITURGIES FOR YEAR C ❧
VOLUME I

EDITED BY

Kimberly Bracken Long

WJK WESTMINSTER
JOHN KNOX PRESS
LOUISVILLE · KENTUCKY

First edition

Published by Westminster John Knox Press
Louisville, Kentucky

12 13 14 15 16 17 18 19 20 21—10 9 8 7 6 5 4 3 2 1

Book design by Drew Stevens
Cover design by Lisa Buckley and Dilu Nicholas

Library of Congress Cataloging-in-Publication Data

Feasting on the Word worship companion : liturgies for Year C / edited by
Kimberly Bracken Long. — 1st ed.
  p. cm.
 Includes index.
 ISBN 978-0-664-23805-6 (alk. paper)
 1. Common lectionary (1992) 2. Lectionaries. 3. Worship programs.
 I. Long, Kimberly Bracken.
 BV199.L42F43 2012
 264'.13—dc23

                                                    2012011192

PRINTED IN THE UNITED STATES OF AMERICA

∞ The paper used in this publication meets the minimum requirements
of the American National Standard for Information Sciences—Permanence of Paper
for Printed Library Materials, ANSI Z39.48-1992.

Westminster John Knox Press advocates the responsible use of our natural resources. The text paper of this book is made from 30% post-consumer waste.

Most Westminster John Knox Press books are available at special quantity discounts when purchased in bulk by corporations, organizations, and special-interest groups. For more information, please e-mail SpecialSales@wjkbooks.com.

Contents

LENT

HOLY WEEK

EASTER

ADDITIONAL RESOURCES

Introduction

The *Feasting on the Word Worship Companion* offers language for the church's worship for every Sunday and holy day in the Revised Common Lectionary for Years A, B, and C. It is intended to serve as a supplement to the liturgical resources of denominations and not as a substitute for any of those fine works. This first volume provides liturgy for Year C, Advent through Pentecost.

The texts herein were written by people from five ecclesial bodies who share similar convictions about worship and its language, yet pray with distinct voices. Because the writers come from a range of Protestant traditions, the attentive reader will notice some differences in theological background; in every case, however, these texts are grounded in deep and careful theological reflection. We seek to offer liturgy that is accessible yet elegant, in words that are poetic but not overwrought. These texts are written for the ear; we hope they are easily spoken, and their meanings quickly apprehended, in order to encourage full and rich congregational participation in the church's life of prayer.

These words are rooted in Scripture, as the church's liturgies have been for centuries. Using the Revised Common Lectionary as a guide, the writers of this volume offer words for worship that do not merely spring from their own imaginations but are grounded in the Word of God.

What This Book Includes

— Prayers and other liturgical texts—from Opening Words to Blessing—
   for every Sunday and holy day through Pentecost (Year C)
— A collection of greetings to be used at the beginning of a worship
   service

- Thanksgivings for Baptism, for use at the beginning of a worship service or for reaffirmation of baptism
- Prayers for Communion, or Eucharist, for Sundays throughout the Christian year
- Questions for reflection on the texts for each Sunday and holy day
- Morning and evening prayers for household use, to be prayed by individuals, families, or groups, based on the week's lectionary readings. (These prayers are written in both singular and plural, so adapt them as needed.) These may be distributed throughout a congregation for use during the week as a way to continue reflecting on the Sunday texts.
- A CD-ROM, which enables worship planners to copy text and paste it in the worship bulletin. Permission is granted to reprint individual prayers and liturgical texts for worship provided that the following notice is included: Reprinted by permission of Westminster John Knox Press from *Feasting on the Word® Worship Companion*. Copyright 2012.

Eucharistic prayers are provided in a separate section in acknowledgment that not all Christian churches celebrate the Lord's Supper every Sunday. In addition to two prayers for general use and prayers for holy days are also provided. A congregation that celebrates communion weekly might consider using one eucharistic prayer for a season, or other period of time, to allow people to become familiar with the prayer through repeated use.

How to Use This Book

One may use this book in a variety of ways. You may use the texts just as they are, or you may adapt them for your context. While new texts are offered for each Sunday in Year C, there is value in repeating portions of liturgy so that people might become familiar with them. When worshipers are able to speak the same set of words over a period of time, they are not continually adjusting to new ideas and patterns of speech. You may, for example, use the same prayer of confession for a season, allowing the people to enter more deeply into that prayer over time.

Although a basic fourfold pattern of worship is used here, the elements of worship may not be arranged in the same way they appear in your own church's order of worship. This is not intended to privilege one tradition over another, but simply to arrange the elements in a way that will look familiar to many who use this book.

You will notice that these texts are arranged in "sense lines"—that is, they look more like poems than paragraphs. This is intentional. The eye can pick up phrases quickly, enabling worshipers to pray them with greater understanding. So, if you reproduce any of these texts, please retain the sense lines. This layout on the page also helps leaders to better speak the texts so that they can actually proclaim (and not just read) the texts, while maintaining eye contact with worshipers.

In cases where a congregational response is used, instructions are often included that will allow the prayers to be led without printing them in their entirety.

This book is full of words. Worship, however, does not happen on a page. As you use these texts, do not just read them. Pray them. Spend time with the words and make them your own so that you may lead with authenticity, wisdom, and a true sense of prayer.

A Word about the Lectionary

During Ordinary Time, or the season after Pentecost, liturgy is provided for both the semicontinuous and complementary streams of the Revised Common Lectionary. Each of these tracks uses the same epistle and gospel reading, but the Old Testament and Psalm lections are different. The semicontinuous track allows congregations to read continually through a book of Scripture from week to week. In the complementary track, the Old Testament readings are chosen to relate to (or complement) the Gospel reading of the day. In both cases, the psalm is understood as a response to the Old Testament reading. Liturgical resources for the Season after Pentecost will appear in volumes 2, 4, and 6.

Since the numbering of the Sundays after Pentecost varies from year to year, the designation of "Proper" is used here, as it is in the Feasting on the Word commentaries. It can be confusing to navigate the various ways churches designate Sundays; a handy resource for viewing all those labels in one place can be found at http://lectionary.library.vanderbilt.edu/, a user-friendly site provided to the public by Vanderbilt University.

Different Voices: The Ecumenical Nature of the Project

Each writer comes to his or her task having been formed by a particular liturgical tradition. We are Methodist, Episcopal, United Church of Christ, Presbyterian, and Lutheran, with a variety of backgrounds and experiences.

Working as a team, we chose elements of worship that are common to all of us, as well as some elements that are particular to one church but not necessarily to another. The Presbyterians, for instance, insist on including prayers of confession and prayers for illumination that invoke the Holy Spirit. Lutherans and Episcopalians expect a prayer of the day and include prayers for the departed in the intercessions. Lutherans also commonly use language about law and grace, and declarations of forgiveness sometimes refer to the ordination of the presider. These particularities were retained in order to preserve the ecumenical character of the book.

We use a variety of ways of praying but a consistent pattern of worship elements for each Sunday in the Christian year. Feel free to adapt the forms, change the words, or choose what is best suited for your context.

Who We Are

Just as this book is intended to serve as a companion to *Feasting on the Word: Preaching the Revised Common Lectionary*, we seek to be companions along the way with those of you who plan and lead worship.

The core team of writers includes:

Kimberly L. Clayton, Director of Supervised Ministries at Columbia Theological Seminary, Decatur, Georgia; Presbyterian Church (U.S.A.)

David Gambrell, Associate for Worship in the Office of Theology and Worship of the Presbyterian Church (U.S.A.), Louisville, Kentucky; Presbyterian Church (U.S.A.)

Daniel M. Geslin, Pastor of Sixth Avenue United Church of Christ, Denver, Colorado; United Church of Christ

Kimberly Bracken Long, Assistant Professor of Worship, Columbia Theological Seminary, Decatur, Georgia; Presbyterian Church (U.S.A.)

L. Edward Phillips, Associate Professor of Worship and Liturgical Theology, Candler School of Theology, Atlanta, Georgia; United Methodist Church

Melinda Quivik, Liturgical Scholar, Houghton, Michigan; Evangelical Lutheran Church in America

Carol L. Wade, Dean of Christ Church Cathedral, Lexington, Kentucky; Episcopal Church

Other contributors include:

Jennifer Carlier, Decatur, Georgia
Marissa Galvan-Valle, Louisville, Kentucky
Kathryn Schneider Halliburton, Colorado Springs, Colorado
L'Anni Hill, Decatur, Georgia
Elizabeth C. Knowlton, Atlanta, Georgia
Franklin E. Lewis, Chester, West Virginia
Elizabeth H. Shannon, St. Petersburg, Florida
Margaret LaMotte Torrence, Asheville, North Carolina

The generosity of many people has helped bring this work to fruition. David Maxwell, executive editor of Westminster John Knox Press has provided gentle guidance, shown great wisdom, and shared his seemingly boundless good humor. David Dobson, editorial director of WJK has offered constant support and encouragement. Columbia Theological Seminary provided meeting space, hospitality, and encouragement for the project.

No words are sufficient to describe the depth of God's grace or beautiful enough to address to the creator of the cosmos. We offer these words with the prayer that they might be useful to the church in enabling worshiping communities to stammer forth their thanks and praise.

Kimberly Bracken Long

First Sunday of Advent

Jeremiah 33:14–16   1 Thessalonians 3:9–13
Psalm 25:1–10   Luke 21:25–36

OPENING WORDS / CALL TO WORSHIP

The days are surely coming, says the LORD,   *Jer. 33:14–16*
when I will fulfill my promise to my people.
Justice and righteousness will fill the land
and all will live in peace and safety.

[or]

There will be signs in the heavens   *Luke 21:25–36*
and distress among the nations.
When Christ returns in power and glory
people will faint with fear.
But when you see these things, lift up your heads:
our redemption is drawing near!
Heaven and earth may pass away,
but the Word of God will stand unshaken.

CALL TO CONFESSION

Jesus said, Do not let your hearts be weighed down   *Luke 21:25–36*
by the sins and worries of this life,
but watch and pray for the grace of God,
who will save you in your time of trial.
With confidence in God's mercy,
let us confess our sin.

PRAYER OF CONFESSION

Lord, have mercy on us.
We are not ready for your coming.
We live in sin,
as though there were no justice.

1

We live in fear,
as though there were no grace.
Forgive us, Lord. *Ps. 25:4–6*
Show us your mercy and steadfast love.
Lead us in your truth, and teach us your paths,
for you are the God of our salvation. Amen.

DECLARATION OF FORGIVENESS
Friends, believe the good news:
In Jesus Christ you are forgiven.
Thanks be to God.

May the Lord guide your way, *1 Thess. 3:9–13*
strengthen you in all holiness,
and make you abound in love
for one another and for all.

PRAYER OF THE DAY
Holy One, you have promised us
that the day of our salvation is near.
Keep us faithful in love and watchful in prayer,
so that we may stand with confidence and joy
at the coming of Christ, our redeemer and Lord. **Amen.**

PRAYER FOR ILLUMINATION
God our salvation, *Ps. 25:1–10*
there is wisdom, peace, and joy
for those who keep your Word.
By the power of your Holy Spirit,
lead us in your truth
and teach us to do your will;
for the sake of Jesus Christ our Lord. **Amen.**

PRAYERS OF INTERCESSION
[A brief silence may follow each petition.]
Let us pray to the Lord, saying,
   in your mercy, Lord, save us.

Merciful God,
you call us to goodness and lead us on right paths.

You encourage us with signs of your coming
and urge us to keep watch,
that we might greet you with heads raised high
when you come to restore all of creation.
Watching and waiting, we pray for this world that needs
    your saving power.

For nations at war,
    in your mercy, **Lord, save us.**
For all who suffer from violence, in the streets or in their homes,
    in your mercy, **Lord, save us.**
For all who live in worry or fear,
    in your mercy, **Lord, save us.**
For those who have forgotten the ways of righteousness,
    in your mercy, **Lord, save us.**
For those who have never heard of your rescuing love,
    in your mercy, **Lord, save us.**
For all those who have lost hope, or never had it at all,
    in your mercy, **Lord, save us.**

We pray, too, for your church in the world,
that we may increase in ardor for you and your children,
and work in confidence for your coming reign.
Now by the power of your Holy Spirit, make us ever more faithful,
that we may greet you in confidence and joy on that great day;
    through Christ, in whose name we pray. **Amen.**

INVITATION TO THE OFFERING
Trusting in the sure promises of Christ,
and grateful for the Spirit's sustaining power,
let us bring our tithes and offerings to God.

PRAYER OF THANKSGIVING/DEDICATION
God of righteousness,
you have saved us from the worst the world can do
and have promised to redeem the whole creation when
    Christ comes again.
In faith and hope we offer our gifts of money and self,
that we may be part of what you are doing in the world even now,
as we watch for Christ's coming in glory. **Amen.**

CHARGE

> Go in peace,
> live in love,
> and seek to be holy in all that you do.

BLESSING

> May the God of mercy keep you,
> the Holy Spirit cheer you,
> and Christ in glory greet you,
> now and at the day of his coming.

Question for Reflection

Even in the midst of trouble and turmoil, God allows us glimpses of the kingdom to come. What signs of promise do you see that bolster your hope in a new heaven and a new earth?

Household Prayer: Morning

Thank you for this new day to sing your praise
and watch for signs of your kingdom.
By your Spirit, let me abound in love for you and your children,
that in living and loving I may point to your coming reign.
In the name of Jesus I pray. Amen.

Household Prayer: Evening

Thank you for the signs of your coming reign,
and for the power of your saving love.
Bless all those whom I met today,
and strengthen their hope in your power and grace.
Now as I close my eyes,
I relinquish all anxieties and fears,
trusting in your providence and mercy. Amen.

Second Sunday of Advent

Baruch 5:1–9 *or* Malachi 3:1–4   Philippians 1:3–11
Luke 1:68–79   Luke 3:1–6

OPENING WORDS / CALL TO WORSHIP
John came out of the wilderness to preach repentance;
he preaches to us still.
Make straight the paths we now walk
and prepare the way for God's reign of justice and love.

CALL TO CONFESSION
Saints, let us trust in God's love for us and confess our sin,
confident in God's mercy.

PRAYER OF CONFESSION
Refining God, you have sent us prophets and we have not listened.
We have not always determined what is best
or made way for your reign
in our lives, our church, and our society.
Forgive us, we pray, and renew your covenant within us,
for the sake of Jesus Christ, our Lord. Amen.

DECLARATION OF FORGIVENESS
Friends, I am confident of this:
if we repent, God is sure to forgive us.
The One who began a good work in us will bring it to completion.
Grateful for the promise of joy and of peace,
let us share that peace with one another.

PRAYER OF THE DAY

Covenant God,
you send us messengers
to cleanse and refine us for your coming.
Help us endure the mirror of the prophets' message,
that we may see you
when you suddenly appear among us;
through Jesus Christ. **Amen.**

PRAYER FOR ILLUMINATION

Holy One, through your Holy Spirit
instruct us by the light of your prophets.
Illumine our hearts, that we may hear your call
to become your path into the world.
In the name of Jesus Christ we pray. **Amen.**

PRAYERS OF INTERCESSION

[A brief time of silence may be kept after each intercession.]
Loving God, through the gift of prayer   *Phil. 1:7*
you teach us to hold one another in our hearts.

Hear now our prayers:

for the leaders and people of every nation:	*Luke 3:1*
for the church and all who serve the Lord:	*Luke 3:2*
for those who suffer in sorrow and affliction:	*Bar. 5:1*
for refugees and travelers far from home:	*Bar. 5:5–7*
for all who are in prison or facing trial:	*Phil. 1:7*
for those who sit in darkness, or in the shadow of death:	*Luke 1:79*

Gracious God, this is our prayer:
that your love will overflow more and more   *Phil. 1:9, 8*
in our lives, in your church, and in all the world,
until all may know the compassion of Christ Jesus,
our Savior and Lord, in whose name we pray. **Amen.**

INVITATION TO THE OFFERING

We are called by God to present a harvest
   of righteousness—   *Phil. 1:11, 6*
not by virtue of our own works,
but by the grace of the one who began a good work in us,
and is even now bringing it to completion.
Let us bring the offerings of our lives to the Lord.

PRAYER OF THANKSGIVING/DEDICATION

God of all righteousness,   *Mal. 3:1-4*
receive these gifts of gratitude,
the offerings of our lives.
Purify them with your refining fire
so that they may serve your purposes
and shine with your glory;
through Jesus Christ our Lord. **Amen.**

CHARGE

I am confident of this: *Phil. 1:6*
that the one who began a good work in you
will bring it to completion by the day of Jesus Christ.
Prepare the way of the Lord!   *Luke 3:4*

BLESSING

The grace of the Lord Jesus Christ be with your spirit.   *Phil. 4:23*

Questions for Reflection

The prophet Malachi says that God is "like a refiner's fire and like fuller's soap" (Mal. 3:2). Reflect on events of the past year. How has God been working to refine and purify your life or your community of faith?

Paul writes to the church at Philippi: "I thank my God every time I remember you, constantly praying with joy in every one of my prayers for all of you, because of your sharing in the gospel from the first day until now" (Phil.1:3–5). Think about people in your life for whom you give thanks, who have been in your prayers, and who have brought good news and joy to you this year. Consider writing them a letter or card to express your gratitude.

Household Prayer: Morning

Blessed are you, Lord God: *Luke 1:68, 78–79*
by your tender mercy
the dawn breaks upon us.
Guide our feet this day
in paths of peace;
through Jesus Christ our Lord. Amen.

Household Prayer: Evening

Blessed are you, Lord God: *Luke 1:68, 79*
for you have smiled on us this day
and redeemed us from our sin.
Give light to all who wait in darkness
until we rest with you in perfect peace;
through Jesus Christ our Lord. Amen.

Third Sunday of Advent

Zephaniah 3:14–20   Philippians 4:4–7
Isaiah 12:2–6   Luke 3:7–18

OPENING WORDS / CALL TO WORSHIP
>Give thanks to the Lord and call upon the holy name
>>of the most high God.   *Isa. 12:2-3*
>**The Lord is our strength and our salvation.**
>Proclaim the mercy of the One who comes as one of us.
>**The Lord is our strength and our salvation.**
>Trust and do not be afraid.
>**The Lord is our strength and our salvation.**
>With joy you will draw water from the wells of peace.
>**The Lord is our strength and our salvation. Hallelujah! Amen.**

CALL TO CONFESSION
>As John the Baptist called the people to repent,
>as Jesus calls us now,
>we turn to the one who is both judge and savior,
>trusting that repentance opens the door to new life,
>and that peace beyond all measure has been promised to us.
>Let us confess our sins.
>*[time for silent confession]*

PRAYER OF CONFESSION
>The Lord is near.
>**In your presence, Holy God,**
>**we confess that we need repentance.**
>**We have broken your commands against idolatry.**
>**We do not live in peace with your creation or your people.**
>**We have not trusted your word, and we are afraid.**
>**Forgive us, restore us, and turn our shame into praise,**

9

for the sake of the One who proclaims the good news
and for the sake of all the world. Amen.

DECLARATION OF FORGIVENESS

In the name of the one God
who lives and moves among us,
you are forgiven.
The Lord has taken away the judgments against you.   *Zeph. 3:15*
Do not worry.
Live in peace.

PRAYER OF THE DAY

Merciful God,
you come into our midst
longing for communion with us,
becoming one of us.
Break our resistance to life with you,
show us the path toward just relations,
and bring us into your unimaginable peace;
in Jesus' name. **Amen.**

PRAYER FOR ILLUMINATION

Holy Word,
you are our guide and ultimate assurance.
By your Holy Spirit,
open us to your promises and commands
and shower us again with the fire of your love. **Amen.**

PRAYERS OF INTERCESSION

Let us offer our prayers of intercession to God, saying,
God, you are in our midst, renew us in your love.

Lord of Life, you call us to prepare the way for your reign
by bearing fruit worthy of repentance.
You lift up a vision before us of a world that is shared and fair,
where needs are met and no one is outcast.
Baptize us fresh in your Spirit as we pray,
God, you are in our midst, **renew us in your love.**

We pray for the nations of the world,
both allies and enemies,
for their leaders and their people.
Make yourself known to us all,
that all the peoples of the earth may live in justice and peace.
    God, you are in our midst, **renew us in your love.**

For your church here and abroad,
that we hear your call for justice as good news for all people.
    God, you are in our midst, **renew us in your love.**

We pray for peace in our world,
especially for those caught in war,
and for all who live in fear of violence, extortion, threats,
        and false accusations.
    God, you are in our midst, **renew us in your love.**

For those who suffer from natural disasters,
from hunger and cold.
Lead us to share our food and our coats with them.
    God, you are in our midst, **renew us in your love.**

For the frail, the sick, and all those whose hands grow weak,
lead us to help them with gentleness.
    God, you are in our midst, **renew us in your love.**

For those who are disabled, oppressed, or outcast among us,
change their pain into praise, and let their courage be renowned
        in the world.
    God, you are in our midst, **renew us in your love.**

For the earth from which we draw our health, our strength,
        our inspiration,
and for all the living creatures in whose community we live—
    God, you are in our midst, **renew us in your love.**

Surely, God, we can trust in you and not be afraid.
Lead us in songs of praise and shouts of joy, for you are in our midst.
We pray through the one who baptizes us not only with water
but with the Holy Spirit, now and forever. **Amen.**

INVITATION TO THE OFFERING

Let us bring to God our offerings,
with thanksgiving that God provides more than enough for all.
Let us give, as each is able, for the benefit of Christ's church and
     God's world.

PRAYER OF THANKSGIVING/DEDICATION

Gracious God, in gratitude for all that you have given us,
we bring our tithes, offerings, and labor
to help feed a world hungry for healing and hope;
for the sake of Jesus Christ. **Amen.**

CHARGE

Go to love and serve the Lord,
showing mercy to all.

BLESSING

May the peace of God,   *Phil. 4:7*
which passes all understanding,
guard your hearts and your minds in Christ Jesus,
for whom we watch and wait.

Questions for Reflection

Imagine that you are in the crowd listening to John the Baptizer. You hear
people in the crowd asking him, "What should we do to prepare?" How
might John instruct you, or your church, to prepare for the coming of
God's reign?

Sometimes wealthy people worry that God or the church is requiring them
to be poor. What is the difference between being poor and being fair? How
do you feel about sharing?

Household Prayer: Morning

God, surely you are my salvation.
I begin this day without fear, trusting you,
for you are my strength.

Help me to meditate all day
on the thought that you are rejoicing in me!
And keep me keenly aware, as I travel through this day,
of ways that I may help others, especially those with special needs.
Then bring me home to you at the close of the day. Amen.

Household Prayer: Evening

Thank you, God, for the gift of today
and for guarding my heart and my mind in Christ Jesus.
All that I did and all that I left undone,
I now give over to your safekeeping,
trusting in your peace that surpasses all understanding.
Be my rest as I sleep tonight,
and renew me in your love for another day. Amen.

Fourth Sunday of Advent

Micah 5:2–5a   Hebrews 10:5–10
Luke 1:47–55 *or* Psalm 80:1–7   Luke 1:39–45 (46–55)

OPENING WORDS / CALL TO WORSHIP
Out of little Bethlehem comes one who is to rule in Israel.
He shall be great to the ends of the earth.
Our spirits rejoice in God our Savior.
God's mercy extends from generation to generation.
Holy is God's name!
[or]
Not in the mighty places of power,
but in little Bethlehem,
in a room out back:
The Messiah is coming.

Not born in nobility and wealth,
but of Mary and Joseph,
who pondered and planed wood:
The Messiah is coming.

Not announced by prophets, priests, and kings,
but by two women,
who were the first to know:
The Messiah is coming.

Nothing will be impossible for God,
but when and where we least expect it,
look among the straw and the stars:
The Messiah is coming.

CALL TO CONFESSION

In the world, and in this season, there are many claims on our lives.
We take this time to remember that in our baptism, Christ claimed
    us as his own.
We acknowledge before God and one another
that we have not followed Jesus Christ with all our heart and mind
    and strength.
Trusting in God's grace, let us pray.

PRAYER OF CONFESSION

God our Savior, we ask for your mercy.
Though we have heard Mary's song,
we still seek security in pride and power and possessions.
Though we know your story,
we resist the costs of following you.
We pass by those considered lowly in this world.
We turn away from hungry people who still wait to be filled.
Forgive us, we pray.
Help us to work for the justice you intend.
Make us messengers of the peace you bring.
As we wait for you, turn our apathy into acts of love and service.
We pray in the name of Jesus Christ, Emmanuel. Amen.

DECLARATION OF FORGIVENESS

Friends, God is for us and not against us.
For that very reason, God sent the Son into the world—
not to condemn the world,
but that the world might be saved through him.
Believe the good news:
In Jesus Christ, we are forgiven!

PRAYER OF THE DAY

Stir up your power, O God,
and come to set us free
by the righteousness of your birth in our midst,
by the light of your face shining upon us,
and by becoming our brother, our friend, our salvation.
We pray this in the name of the Holy Trinity:
Father, Son, and Holy Spirit,
one God, mother of us all. **Amen.**

PRAYER FOR ILLUMINATION

O Mighty One,
who scatters the proud
and fills the hungry,
by your Holy Spirit
let your word leap in us
and bring to our yearning
the joy that comes with
new beginnings and renewed lives. **Amen.**

PRAYERS OF INTERCESSION

Let us pray to the Lord, saying,
Hear us, O God. Your mercy is great.

Holy God, you reveal yourself in so many ways,
especially in your son, Jesus Christ.
We gather up the prayers of this community
for the church, the world, and all in need,
confident that you know our deepest thoughts
and will refresh our spirits.
We pray in the name of the One
who transforms principalities and powers
and renews the heavens and the earth,
Christ our Savior.
Hear us, O God. **Your mercy is great.**

For the church:
We pray for our sisters and brothers in Christ
who gather as we do on this day all over the world
in house churches and storefronts,
on reservations, in townships and base communities,
among immigrants, in hospital chapels and prisons,
and with persons who are dying.
Wherever the church is found on frontiers of mission and service,
empower its witness to strengthen and stretch the vision of your people.
Hear us, O God. **Your mercy is great.**

For the earth and all creatures:
We pray for the healing and well-tending of all that you have given us;
for water and air, soil and stars;

for creatures that roam the seas and those that fly thousands of
    miles in migration;
for mammals and reptiles,
insects and microbes in swamps and forests and in our own homes.
Show us their beauty and our need for them.
Hear us, O God. **Your mercy is great.**

For an end to violence, oppression, and injustice:
We pray for all who sing with Mary a song of joy for deliverance;
for all people who long to hear your promise of good news;
for all peacemakers;
for governments that hold at the heart of their work
the needs of people otherwise invisible;
for all people left homeless and destitute by the greed of others.
Lead your people from darkness to light.
    Hear us, O God. **Your mercy is great.**

For Mary and Joseph in every land:
We pray for all people who face the enormous vocation of raising
    children;
for biological parents and adopting parents,
for grandparents, aunts, uncles, cousins, and friends;
for children who long for a parent's or guardian's love and care;
for children who will be born today;
and especially for those born into hunger and insecurity.
Let the light of your desire for our well-being shine through all children.
    Hear us, O God. **Your mercy is great.**

For those we hold dear
and those who have asked for our prayers:
We pray for everyone who is in any need today:
for the lonely;
for all people who are anxious at this time of year;
for our elders in the nursing home;
for people who cannot find work
and those whose work is not life-giving for them;
for . . . *[names kept by the church for remembrance on Sunday]* and for
    those we name now either out loud or in our hearts . . .
[names may be called forth from the assembly].
    Hear us, O God. **Your mercy is great.**

For our own lives:
We pray that Mary's song of joy and Joseph's loyalty will be
    magnified in us.
Fill us with the breath of Advent.
Stir us to extend ourselves beyond what we thought possible.
Show us that like Mary, we need not fear.
    Hear us, O God. **Your mercy is great.**

We remember with thanksgiving the faithful who have gone before us,
especially . . . *[names of those recently deceased and those saints whose
commemoration day falls in the week ahead may be named].* As your
light shines on us through them, guide us to so enlighten others.
    Hear us, O God. **Your mercy is great.**

With the whole church, we cry "Let it be," trusting in your word. **Amen.**

INVITATION TO THE OFFERING

God does not desire us to bring burnt offerings and
    sin offerings,   *Heb. 10:5–10*
but instead asks that we do God's will.
So we bring to God now the offerings of our lives
    and our labors,
with the prayer that God's will may be done
    through them.

PRAYER OF THANKSGIVING/DEDICATION

You deliver us, O God,
from exile, separation, and despair
into communion with each other, with you, and with your good news.
We thank you for all that draws us close together,
astounding us with lives transformed by gratitude.
Accept our gifts as signs of our gratitude
for what you give us every day
and as honor to your presence in our world;
for the sake of those who stand in need
and Jesus Christ, who saves us. **Amen.**

CHARGE

Go in peace,
trusting in the promises of God.

BLESSING

May the God of justice be your path,
the Lord of mercy be your guide,
and the Spirit of love be your light,
this day and forevermore.

Question for Reflection

Where do you see the light of Christ magnified in your person, your life, and the ways of your family and community? Notice in the coming week one time each day when the light of Christ is made present for you by others.

Household Prayer: Morning

Thank you, good and gracious God,
for the morning light,
for another day in which to
live out what it means that you have magnified my soul
and the souls of those around me in this world.
Teach me the meaning of "Let it be."
Show me how to trust;
in Jesus' name. Amen.

Household Prayer: Evening

Good and gracious God,
we give you thanks that
you have made incarnate in your world
the breath of life,
the life of hope.
Keep us safe throughout the night
that in the morning we may again rejoice
and live in peace with all creation;
in Jesus' name. Amen.

Nativity of the Lord /
Proper I / Christmas Eve

Isaiah 9:2–7   Titus 2:11–14
Psalm 96   Luke 2:1–14 (15–20)

OPENING WORDS / CALL TO WORSHIP
  Rejoice! I bring good news for all people.
  Unto us a child is born. Alleluia!
  Tonight the angels sing on earth.
  Glory to God in the highest!
[or]
  Behold! I bring good news for all people.
  Unto us a child is born this night,
  a Savior, Christ the Lord.   *Luke 2:10–11*

[To highlight the tone of Christmas celebration, it is appropriate to omit the confession and pardon on this occasion. A Gloria or other brief song of praise may be sung. Elements of penitential petition and pardon can be included in the Prayers of the People. Alternatively, the following may be used.]

  Jesus, you are God's holy child, born of Mary:
  Lord have mercy.

  Jesus, in you all the fullness of God is pleased to dwell.
  Christ have mercy.

  Jesus, you are the Word made flesh, full of grace and truth.
  Lord have mercy.

PRAYER OF THE DAY
  Eternal God,
  from the tabernacle of heaven to the poverty of a stable,
  your radiant light shines forth in a tiny baby wrapped in rags;

such humble Love astounds us.
In Jesus you have become one with us
that we might become one with you.
Open our hearts to joyfully receive his love
that he may be born in us, and we in him,
through Christ our Lord. **Amen.**

PRAYER FOR ILLUMINATION

Glorious God, in Jesus your grace appears, *Titus 2:11*
bringing salvation to all.
Help us to ponder your words of love by the light of your Spirit,
that we may proclaim glad tidings of peace
and welcome Christ in our world. **Amen.**

PRAYERS OF INTERCESSION

Gracious and Holy God,
On this night, we have heard how the world into which Jesus was born
was ruled by governor, emperor, and king.
Yet this story reveals that you, O God,
are the only true Sovereign—Almighty and Everlasting.
We thank you that justice and righteousness are in your hands.
We praise you for the peace you have promised.
Most especially, we thank you for your Son, Jesus Christ,
the Light of the world,
who dwells among us full of grace and truth.

Hear now our prayers of intercession,
that all people might find healing, comfort, and joy.

We pray for public officials, rulers, and leaders in our own time:
Give them wisdom in decrees and decisions,
a will for the common good,
and the courage to work for peace in local communities and among
    the nations . . .

Shine upon them and give them peace.

We pray for all who work and watch this night:
for those in hospitals and positions of public service;
for those serving our country here and around the globe;

for those in airports, trains, and bus stations;
for those who work in shelters, hotels, and other places of hospitality . . .

Shine upon them and give them peace.

We pray for all who suffer this night:
those who are sick and those who are dying;
for one who is cold;
for one who is lonely or grieving;
for people who are hungry and thirsty;
for all who struggle with addiction . . .

Shine upon them and give them peace.

We pray for families and friends:
for those who are with us and those far away;
for those who are traveling;
for those who especially need your guidance in this season;
and for those in our memories who now dwell with you . . .

Shine upon them and give them peace.

We pray, O God, with the multitude of the heavenly host,
that through Jesus Christ your glory will lighten every darkness;
that your peace will fill all in all.
We pray that those who live in the midst of war
may instead live without fear and destruction;
that those who live with the threat of danger in homes
or on city streets may instead dwell in safety;
and that all your creatures, and creation itself,
may be restored and renewed.

Shine upon them and give them peace.

Conform our prayers to your will,
and use us to accomplish your purposes,
for the sake of Jesus Christ. **Amen.**

INVITATION TO THE OFFERING

The grace of God has appeared, bringing salvation to all.
Jesus Christ has shown us how to live:
loving God and neighbor,
sharing what we have,
engaging in acts of mercy and justice.
As we celebrate his birth,
and wait in hope for his coming again,
let us bring the offerings of our lives before him.

PRAYER OF THANKSGIVING/DEDICATION

God of every good and perfect gift,
we thank you for your greatest gift,
your Son, Jesus Christ our Lord.
In this season when so many gifts are given and received,
we pray that you will receive the gifts we offer now.
Use them according to your purposes and plans,
bringing your good news of great joy to all people;
through Jesus Christ, our Savior. **Amen.**

CHARGE

Go into the night,   *Luke 2:20*
glorifying and praising God for all you have seen
    and heard.

BLESSING

May Christ be your light,
this night and forevermore.

Questions for Reflection

Isaiah names the one who will come to rule: Wonderful Counselor, Mighty God, Everlasting Father, Prince of Peace. Do these names for God, made known in Jesus Christ, describe your own experience of God? Is there a particular time when God seemed especially near to you as one of these names? This Christmas Eve, as you reflect on the circumstances in the world, which name for God would you choose to call upon in prayer?

Household Prayer: Morning

Prince of Peace,
On this morning before Christmas,
I pray for an abiding sense of your peace,
in my life and in the lives of those I love.
I pray, too, for peace to come into every troubled heart,
home, and community.
This day may be rushed and busy,
as it must have been in Bethlehem long ago.
Let there be peace enough in my heart and mind
to receive your good news,
in light; in word; in song; in the faces of others.
In peace, help me to treasure the blessings of this day
and ponder your wondrous love. Amen.

Household Prayer: Evening

Wonderful Counselor,
As Christmas Eve draws to an end,
I ready myself to close my eyes and sleep,
to rest in the peace and confidence of your love.
May all the weary world lie down in peace,
confident that your love will break the darkness
as surely as the sun rises each new morning.
Thank you for memories that warm me this night.
I praise you for the gifts that have blessed and sustained me all day.
I entrust myself and those I love to your care,
until we wake in the morning light of Christmas joy—
to greet Jesus Christ our Lord. Amen.

Nativity of the Lord/ Proper III / Christmas Day

Isaiah 52:7–10   Hebrews 1:1–4 (5–12)
Psalm 98   John 1:1–14

OPENING WORDS / CALL TO WORSHIP

For a child has been born for us,
a son given to us;
authority rests upon his shoulders;
and he is named Wonderful Counselor, Mighty God,
Everlasting Father, Prince of Peace.   *Isa. 9:6*
[or]
The people who walked in darkness have seen a great light.
**Those who lived in a land of deep darkness—on them
    light has shined.**   *Isa. 9:2*
The light shines in the darkness.
And the darkness did not overcome it.   *John 1:5*
For Christ is born in Bethlehem.
Come, let us adore him.

CALL TO CONFESSION

As we celebrate the birth of Christ our Savior,
let us acknowledge our failure to receive him fully into our world,
trusting in the mercy of God.

PRAYER OF CONFESSION

Almighty God,
we confess that our hearts have not been open
to all that you have revealed to us in the Nativity of your Son.
You sent Christ to be born as a helpless Child,
and yet we have not attended to suffering of children.
You chose humble Mary to be mother of our Lord Jesus,
and yet we have not attended to the struggles of women.

The holy family could find no room in Bethlehem but a stable,
and yet we have not attended to the cry of the homeless.
You announced your birth to lowly shepherds,
yet we ignore those who tend our farms and fields.
Forgive our lack of attention,
and free us for joyful compassion,
that we may know Christ in serving others.
Though Jesus Christ we pray. Amen.

DECLARATION OF FORGIVENESS

Isaiah foretold the good news that is now proclaimed to us:
The Lord has comforted the people   *Isa. 52:9b*
and redeemed Jerusalem.
In the name of Jesus Christ, we are forgiven.

PRAYER OF THE DAY

Almighty God,
Christ your Word became flesh and dwelt among us,
born in Bethlehem.
May we receive Christ into our lives
and become, through him, your blessed children
who walk in the light you have sent into our world.
Through Christ we pray. **Amen.**

PRAYER FOR ILLUMINATION

Holy God,
through the power of your Holy Spirit
illumine your word,
that we might see Christ,
the living Word,
the light of the world. **Amen.**

PRAYERS OF INTERCESSION

Sisters and brothers,
in Jesus, God's Word became flesh
to birth love in our hearts and peace in our world.
As we celebrate this gift of life in Christ,
let us pray for the church and the world saying,
O God of Love, draw us together in peace.

Your messenger announces peace in shouts of breathless joy;
drive out the warring ways of our world
and protect all who face danger this day
as you guide our feet to travel with the One who is your peace.
O God of Love, **draw us together in peace.**

Your Word comes with justice to rule the earth with fairness;
inspire the leaders of all nations and citizens of the world
to order our economic lives
to promote dignity and equality for all in your global household.
O God of Love, **draw us together in peace.**

Mountains and rivers clap and sing
as your Word makes all things new;
awaken us to the damage we do to your world
and mend our ways,
that all creation might breathe again the liveliness of your blessing.
O God of Love, **draw us together in peace.**

When shepherds met your newborn Christ
they eagerly ran to tell the news;
make us joyful messengers of your good news
who freely share your love in the world.
O God of Love, **draw us together in peace.**

In Jesus, your love takes on human form
to seek us out and guide us home;
may Christ be born in us today
to lead us into the lives for which we were made.
O God of Love, **draw us together in peace.**

From your majesty on high to the lowliness of the stable,
your Word has power to sustain all things,
and through him we become your precious children;
comfort those who are hungry, sick, or suffering,
and in all our afflictions anoint us with the oil of gladness
as you visit us with your salvation.
O God of Love, **draw us together in peace.**

Unto us a child is born this day, to live and die and rise again;
bless all who are born today and all who will die,
that your will for them may be fulfilled
in the one who is the way, truth, and life.
O God of Love, **draw us together in peace.**

O God, receive our prayers
through Christ who is our glorious light.
May we, like him, shine forth like the sun
in bodies, breath, and beating hearts
to sing your praise forevermore,
and as holy partners in a heavenly calling,
dwell with you eternally. **Amen.**

INVITATION TO OFFERING

Rejoice! For I bring good news and great joy to all people:
today is born to you a Savior,
Jesus Christ the Lord.
Let us with gladness present the offerings
of our life and labor to the Lord.

PRAYER OF THANKSGIVING/DEDICATION

On this glad new day for all the earth
we are grateful for giving hearts made joyful
in the gift of your Son.
For you, O God, are generosity itself.
Bless these gifts we offer to the benefit of those in need.
Bless our lives in service of sharing your love in the world;
through Jesus Christ we pray. **Amen**

CHARGE

God's Word has come to earth to bring us together in love.
Go in peace to love and serve Christ. Alleluia, alleluia!
Thanks be to God. Alleluia, alleluia!

BLESSING

May the song of the angels,
the joy of the shepherds,
and the peace of the Christ child
be with you this day and always.

Question for Reflection

The Word became flesh and dwelled among us filled with grace and truth. The astonishing mystery of the Incarnation—of God dwelling in bodily form—shows that God loves and blesses us in frail and limited bodies with power to speak love. Where will you embody God's love made known to us in Christ this day?

Household Prayer: Morning

God of small things,
you came among us as a tiny and vulnerable baby
open to all who met you.
Teach us to care for the quiet and tender places
in our hearts and in those of others
as we nurture your compassion in our world. Amen.

Household Prayer: Evening

Creator of the stars of night,
we give you thanks for the love
you have shared with us this day
in the celebration of the birth of Christ.
Blanket us in peace this night as you comfort all in need. Amen.

First Sunday after Christmas

1 Samuel 2:18–20, 26   Colossians 3:12–17
Psalm 148   Luke 2:41–52

OPENING WORDS / CALL TO WORSHIP

Praise the Lord!   *Ps. 148:1, 7, 12*
Praise God in the heavens.
Praise the Lord from the earth!
Young and old alike,
men and women together.
Praise the Lord!

CALL TO CONFESSION

[spoken from the font]
Because we have passed through the waters of baptism,
we dare to bare our souls before God
and reveal the bitterness that dwells in our hearts.
Trusting in God's grace,
let us confess our sin.

PRAYER OF CONFESSION

God of wonder,
you surround us with signs of your glory
and surprise us with your presence,
yet we often miss the marvels you place before us.
Forgive our dullness and make us alert
to the ways you make yourself known,
that we might be witnesses to your good news
and proclaim your extravagant love;
through Jesus Christ, our Savior. Amen

DECLARATION OF FORGIVENESS

[Water may be poured into the font, visibly and audibly.]
In Jesus Christ God saved us,   *Titus 3:5*
not because of any good works that we have done,
but according to God's mercy,
through the water of rebirth and renewal by the Holy Spirit.
People of God, rejoice!
In Jesus Christ, we are forgiven.

As the Lord has forgiven us,   *Col. 3:13*
let us also forgive one another.
The peace of the Lord Jesus Christ be with you.
And also with you.
[The people may share the peace of Christ.]

PRAYER OF THE DAY

O God,
into a realm of clerics and kings
you sent your child
to teach the wise and show the world
what power there is in love.
Keep us vigilant
to hear the voices
of those who speak your truth.
In the name of Jesus we pray. **Amen.**

PRAYER FOR ILLUMINATION

By the breath of your Spirit
inspire us,
that in the hearing of your Word
we may be filled with new understanding
and fresh desire
to please you in all we do,
for the sake of your Son, Jesus. **Amen.**

PRAYERS OF INTERCESSION

Sisters and brothers,
in Jesus, God's Word became flesh
to birth love in our hearts and peace in our world.

As we celebrate this gift of life in Christ,
let us pray for the church and the world saying,
O God of Love, draw us together in peace.

Your messenger announces peace in shouts of breathless joy;
drive out the warring ways of our world
and protect all who face danger this day
as you guide our feet to travel with the One who is your peace.
O God of Love, **draw us together in peace.**

Your Word comes with justice to rule the earth with fairness;
inspire the leaders of all nations and citizens of the world
to order our economic lives
to promote dignity and equality for all in your global household.
O God of Love, **draw us together in peace.**

Mountains and rivers clap and sing
as your Word makes all things new;
awaken us to the damage we do to your world
and mend our ways,
that all creation might breathe again the liveliness of your blessing.
O God of Love, **draw us together in peace.**

When shepherds met your newborn Christ
they eagerly ran to tell the news;
make us joyful messengers of your good news
who freely share your love in the world.
O God of Love, **draw us together in peace.**

In Jesus, your love takes on human form
to seek us out and guide us home;
may Christ be born in us today
to lead us into the lives for which we were made.
O God of Love, **draw us together in peace.**

From your majesty on high to the lowliness of the stable,
your Word has power to sustain all things,
and through him we become your precious children;
comfort those who are hungry, sick, or suffering,

and in all our afflictions anoint us with the oil of gladness
as you visit us with your salvation.
O God of Love, **draw us together in peace.**

Unto us a child is born this day, to live and die and rise again;
bless all who are born today and all who will die,
that your will for them may be fulfilled
in the one who is the way, truth, and life.
O God of Love, **draw us together in peace.**

O God, receive our prayers
through Christ who is our glorious light.
May we, like him, shine forth like the sun
in bodies, breath, and beating hearts
to sing your praise forevermore,
and as holy partners in a heavenly calling,
dwell with you eternally. **Amen.**

INVITATION TO THE OFFERING

With grateful hearts,   *Col. 2:16–17*
let us offer ourselves and our gifts to God,
in the name of the Lord Jesus,
giving thanks to God the Father through him.

PRAYER OF THANKSGIVING/DEDICATION

Loving God:
We give you thanks for Jesus Christ,
the Word made flesh.
Receive the gifts we offer in union with Christ's gift for us.
Clothe us with compassion, kindness, humility,   *Col. 3:14*
meekness, and patience,
that we may be Christ for others.
In his name we pray. **Amen.**

CHARGE

Whatever you do, in word or deed,   *Col. 3:17*
do everything in the name of the Lord Jesus,
giving thanks to God through him.

BLESSING

May the Christ inhabit you,
the Father uphold you,
and the Spirit sustain you,
now and forever.

Questions for Reflection

Consider Jesus as an adolescent, causing his parents to worry about him.
Jesus asks his parents, "Why were you searching for me?" If you were a
parent of Jesus, how would you answer that question? How do you answer
that question for yourself?

Household Prayer: Morning

Lord Jesus, as you listened to your teachers,
may I also, this day, listen to others with care and grace,
and receive whatever wisdom they may offer. Amen.

Household Prayer: Evening

Loving God, you know every struggle I have faced this day:
let me sleep in peace,
confident in your great love in Jesus Christ. Amen.

Second Sunday after Christmas

Jeremiah 31:7–14 *or* Sirach 24:1–12
Psalm 147:12–20 *or*
 Wisdom of Solomon 10:15–21

Ephesians 1:3–14
John 1:(1–9) 10–18

OPENING WORDS / CALL TO WORSHIP

The Word became flesh and lived among us   *John 1:9–14*
And we have seen his glory.
The true light that enlightens everyone
has come into the world.
Glory to God who has blessed us in Christ.
Glory to God forever.

CALL TO CONFESSION

Trusting in God's love made known in the gift of Jesus,
let us confess our sins.

PRAYER OF CONFESSION

Holy God,
we confess that we are a distracted people
and forgetful of your love.
We make selfish choices,
hurt each other, and perpetuate injustice in your world.
We have sinned against you and are deeply sorry
and repent of our disregard of you, each other, and your creation.
By the power of your Spirit,
forgive, restore, and strengthen us
to live in your light and walk in your truth;
through Christ our Lord. Amen.

DECLARATION OF FORGIVENESS

As children of the Holy One,
God forgives you and loves you eternally.

By the power of God's Spirit,
forgive yourself and forgive others
as God in Christ has forgiven you.

PRAYER OF THE DAY
God of glory,
your Word made a home with us
so that we might be at home in you.
Gather your children from the farthest places in the world
and lead us to that home
where the human race can become a human family;
through Jesus Christ and in the Spirit,
one God now and forever. **Amen.**

PRAYER FOR ILLUMINATION
Heavenly Father,
Holy Wisdom came to dwell with us in Jesus,
filling our world with her light and life.
May she also dwell within your word this day,
that we may have intimate knowledge of your love for us,
through the One who is close to your heart,
Jesus Christ your Son. **Amen.**

PRAYERS OF INTERCESSION
God's light breaks through the darkness
to fill our lives with grace and truth.
This is the good news of Christmas;
that Christ came to show us
how to walk the path of wisdom enlightened by your love.
Let us pray for the church and the world saying,
Light of the world, shine in our lives.

Eternal Source,
we pray for Christ's church throughout the world.
May we, like John the Baptist,
point others to the Light in all we do in service of your love.
Light of the world, **shine in our lives.**

Divine Wisdom,
we pray for all leaders of the world.
May your justice guide us to govern
with truth and equity for all.

Prince of Peace,
we pray for all those who live and serve
in places of violence and unrest.
May you keep them from harm's way.

Spirit breath,
we pray for the beauty of creation
witnessed from the vault of heaven to the depths of the sea.
May your goodness stir up in us
a willingness to care for the precious resources
with which you have entrusted us.
Light of the world, **shine in our lives.**

Joy of every human heart,
we pray for all who suffer sickness or sorrow.
May your healing love find a dwelling place
in our lives this day.
Light of the world, **shine in our lives.**

Holy Comforter,
we pray for those in need of food and shelter.
May your abiding presence shelter them with mercy
as we build communities of care.

Eternal Dayspring from on High,
we pray for those who are dying and those who have died.
May they find in you a resting place by springs of living water.

O Great Mystery,
eternity entered time in your Word
and our lives are embraced within the compassion of your Word.
Open our hearts to the Wonder of your love,
that Wisdom may find a home in us and forever speak your praise.
In the name of Jesus Christ we pray. **Amen.**

INVITATION TO THE OFFERING

Christ has lavished upon us the riches of his grace.   *Eph. 1:8*
Therefore, let us offer our lives
and the fruits of our labor to God.

PRAYER OF THANKSGIVING/DEDICATION

Lord Jesus Christ,
your goodness to us is beyond
the reaches of our imagination,
a fullness of love that embraces all of life.
From you we have received grace upon grace.
Accept our offering for the sake of the world.
All that we have is yours,
and all we return to you is but a reflection of your
    love for us.   *John 1:16*
In Jesus' name we pray. **Amen.**

CHARGE

Go forth in the grace of Christ.   *John 1:1–18*
We rejoice in his grace.
Go forth in the light of Christ.
We walk in his light.
Go forth in the love of Christ.
We serve in his love.

BLESSING

May God, the fount of all Wisdom,   *Wis. 10:17*
bless you and guide you
this day and always.

Questions for Reflection

How may I live this day as a child of God who shares in the inheritance of
Christ?

As Christ shines into the darkness of the world around me, what does the
Light of Christ allow me to see?

Household Prayer: Morning

Loving God,
each new day you fill the world
with light for our work and recreation.
As we go to our daily tasks,
teach us to live as your faithful children
whose eyes are open to the light of Christ.
Where there is uncertainty or falsehood,
help us see your truth.
Where there is division or conflict,
keep us in your love.
Enable all that we do or say to bear witness
to our inheritance as children of God;
through Jesus Christ, your beloved Son. Amen.

Household Prayer: Evening

Holy God,
evening falls upon us,
but darkness cannot overcome your light.
In all that we have faithfully accomplished this day,
your light has illumined our way.
In all that we have truthfully spoken this day,
your wisdom has guided our judgment.
In any way we have strayed,
may your light reveal our fault and your wisdom correct our folly.
Let us rest from our labor,
trusting in your love for all your children,
and let us begin tomorrow with renewed strength
to live according to your will.
Through Christ we pray. Amen.

Epiphany of the Lord

Isaiah 60:1–6   Ephesians 3:1–12
Psalm 72:1–7, 10–14   Matthew 2:1–12

OPENING WORDS / CALL TO WORSHIP

Arise, shine; for your light has come.   *Isa. 60:1–3*
The glory of the Lord has risen upon us.
Come, worship the Lord of glory.
Proclaim God's praise among the nations.

CALL TO CONFESSION

In the light of Christ,
we see the shadows of our world and of our hearts.
Trusting in God's grace,
let us confess our sins before God and one another.

PRAYER OF CONFESSION

Merciful God,   *Ps. 72:1–7, 10–14*
you have given light to the world in Jesus Christ,
but we have preferred to live in darkness.
Your justice protects the weak and the distressed,
yet we seek the shelter of privilege and power.
Your righteousness redeems the poor and the needy,
yet we seek the status of wealth and possessions.
Your peace upholds the oppressed and the defenseless,
yet we seek the security of weapons and retribution.
Forgive us our sins, and lead us to true repentance,
that we may trust you in all things;
through Jesus Christ we pray. Amen.

DECLARATION OF FORGIVENESS

This is the good news:
Christ is the light of the world,
who grants forgiveness and healing of our sins.
Thanks be to God.

PRAYER OF THE DAY

God, you placed a star in the sky   *Matt. 2:1–2*
to draw wise folk to the place of Christ's nativity.
There you revealed the mystery
of your eternal purpose for all humanity:
God made flesh, born of Mary,
opening to all the world the promise you made
to Abraham and Sarah.
Empower your church to be as the light of the star,
that we may draw the world
to the glory of Christ, our Lord, through whom we pray. **Amen.**

PRAYER FOR ILLUMINATION

Spirit of God,
in the proclamation of your Word,
reveal to us the hidden mystery of your love in Christ,
and strengthen our faith
that we may approach you with boldness. **Amen.**

PRAYERS OF INTERCESSION

In confidence let us pray to the Lord, saying,
God of Wisdom, Glorious Light, hear our prayer.

Loving God,
Through Christ you call us all
into your covenant with Abraham and Sarah.
For your church throughout the world,
that it may be a faithful witness,
declaring your wisdom to all authorities: *Eph. 3:10*
God of Wisdom, Glorious Light, **hear our prayer.**

The wise men came to King Herod in trust,
but he betrayed their trust and perpetrated unspeakable evil.

For the leaders of the government,
that they reject the way of Herod
and exercise their authority in truth, justice, and mercy:
God of Mercy, Glorious Light, **hear our prayer.**

Joseph, Mary, and Jesus fled before the wrath of Herod
and became refugees in Egypt.
For all those who suffer from political oppression,
injustice, or war, and especially for refugees:
God of Justice, Glorious Light, **hear our prayer.**

Joseph dreamed a future for his son,
and obeyed your will for his family.
For all families that they may live in peace
according to your will,
God of Peace, Glorious Light, **hear our prayer.**

The Holy Family lived with neighbors,
and received help from strangers.
For our neighborhoods,
that they may be communities of human flourishing,
offering kindness to strangers,
God of Harmony, Glorious Light, **hear our prayer.**

Hear our prayers, Gracious God,
and grant us to live as heirs of your promise;
through Jesus Christ our Lord. **Amen.**

INVITATION TO THE OFFERING

God intends to unite all creation,   *Eph. 3:6, 12; Ps. 72:10*
so that all may share in the promises of God's
    new reign.
Therefore with gratitude and joy,
let us render tributes and bring gifts,
for we have access to God in boldness and confidence
though faith in Christ.

PRAYER OF THANKSGIVING/DEDICATION

Glorious God, *Matt. 2:1, 9–11; Eph. 3:6*
you led three men of wisdom
to seek Jesus, your Holy Child, born of Mary.
Overjoyed in the presence of his radiant light,
the men knelt down at the infant's crib
and offered him precious gifts of gold, frankincense,
     and myrrh.
We, too, offer our gifts
in gratitude, reverence, and thanksgiving
for the birth of your child,
whom you called to lead the world into fullness of life.
Receive and bless this offering
as a joyful sign
of the boundless love and abundant life
we are called to share in Christ. **Amen.**

CHARGE

Let us go forth rejoicing in the light of
     God's love. *Isa. 60:1, 5; Matt. 2:10*
Thanks be to God.

BLESSING

May the love of Christ that shines in you
shine brightly in the world wherever you go.
And the blessing of God,
Divine Giver, Radiant Light, and Fountain of Life
bless you and keep you always.

Questions for Reflection

In Epiphany when the magi make their great journey to see the Christ Child, we see Jesus drawing all creation to the divine life revealed in him, and we see the realization of God's dream of reconciled creation. In our own way, we are each endowed by the Spirit with unique and precious gifts for sharing God's healing love in a good but often divided world. What spiritual practices do you engage in that allow you to stay peaceful, courteous, and develop a respectful regard for difference? How do you stay present and create openness for finding, revealing, and activating God's reconciling love in the world?

Household Prayer: Morning

Glorious God,
each day provides opportunity
to awaken to the radiance of your presence,
and to welcome your blessing into my life.
How often I forget that I am your home!
Help me to draw more closely to you,
that I may manifest your love more deeply in the world.
May every bright place and darkened corner
grow ever more luminous as I bear your light this day. Amen.

Household Prayer: Evening

Holy Jesus,
I thank you for sharing your life with me today.
As darkness comes and blankets the earth,
be with all who suffer from sickness, hunger, or lack of shelter.
Kindle in them the warmth of your presence,
and surround them with your steadfast care.
I am grateful for the blessings of this day.
And in the light of your love I rest this night. Amen.

Baptism of the Lord /
First Sunday after the Epiphany

Isaiah 43:1–7	Acts 8:14–17
Psalm 29	Luke 3:15–17, 21–22

OPENING WORDS / CALL TO WORSHIP

The voice of God resounds upon the water. *Ps. 29; Luke 3:21–22*
The Spirit of the Lord hovers over the stream.
The Son of God is named, "Beloved."
And all who worship shout out, "Glory!"
Ascribe to the Lord majesty and strength.
Let us worship God in holy splendor.

CALL TO CONFESSION

God loves us and calls us each by name. *Isa. 43:1*
Knowing we are eternally forgiven and infinitely loved,
let us boldly confess our sins before God.

PRAYER OF CONFESSION

We are precious in your sight, *Isa. 43:4; Luke 3:22*
yet we often forget that we are your beloved.
We confess that our love is fickle and inconstant.
We follow selfish goals
and deny that our way of life harms others and
**   hurts your world.**
We are sorry and we want to change.
Create in us a clean heart,
strengthen our resolve,
reconcile us one to another,
and bless us with your peace. Amen.

DECLARATION OF FORGIVENESS

Beloved, God forgives your sins;
know that you are pardoned
and be at peace to love the Lord and serve the world.

PRAYER OF THE DAY

Holy God, when Jesus was baptized in the Jordan   *Luke 3:21–22*
the heavens opened, the Spirit descended,
and your voice affirmed your love in Jesus
for the healing of the human race and all creation.
By water and word you lovingly invite us
into this same life-giving mission.
May your Spirit,
moving like a stream of water flowing from its source,
work in us this day to realize your vision
of a world made new in Christ,
in whose name we pray. **Amen.**

PRAYER FOR ILLUMINATION

Glorious God,
when Jesus was baptized for your
        healing mission   *Ps. 29:7; Luke 3:21–22*
the heavens opened in a flash of glory
as vision and voice blazed upon the waters.
May your Spirit so burn in us
that we hear your word translated into deed
and follow Jesus in paths of justice, right relationship,
        and peace. **Amen.**

PRAYERS OF INTERCESSION

Glorious God,
as Jesus prayed at his baptism,   *Luke 3:21, 22*
your mothering Spirit brooded over him,
providing sustenance and strength.
So brood over us today
as we offer our prayers for the church and world saying,
Mothering Spirit, stir us with your power.

We pray for your church:
may your word spark our lives with truth and joy

as we serve one another to the glory of your name.
Mothering Spirit, **stir us with your power.**

We pray for all leaders and people around the globe:
may your justice provoke us to shape a peaceful world
where all work for the common good.
Mothering Spirit, **stir us with your power.**

We pray for the well-being of your creation:
may your goodness startle us to the horror of our exploitation
    and abuse.
Mothering Spirit, **stir us with your power.**

We pray for all who suffer grief or sickness of any kind:
may your tender presence abide with us and hasten our healing.
Mothering Spirit, **stir us with your power.**

We pray for all who lack the essentials of life:
may your righteousness raise us up to walk together
with respect and dignity for all.
Mothering Spirit, **stir us with your power.**

We pray for those who have died,
that your steadfast love may shelter them in the peace of your
    eternal light.
Mothering Spirit, **stir us with your power.**

O God, you have made us, formed us,
and called us by name,
and you have redeemed us in Christ.
Receive our prayers this day,
for your life-giving Spirit is powerful to save. **Amen.**

INVITATION TO THE OFFERING
As people who have passed through the waters of baptism,   *Isa. 43:2*
let us make our grateful offering to God our Redeemer.

PRAYER OF THANKSGIVING/DEDICATION
O God,
at his baptism, you acknowledged Jesus as your beloved Son,

and through him you opened to us a way
to become your children by grace.
May these gifts we return to you
be a sign of our dedication to live as your faithful daughters and sons,
born in the waters of baptism by the power of the Holy Spirit;
through Jesus Christ we pray. **Amen.**

CHARGE

We have been with Jesus to the River of Jordan,
river of life, river of promise.
Go forth in the joy of life,
to live as children of promise.

BLESSING

May the grace of our Lord Jesus Christ,
who stood with sinners on the river bank,
uphold you. **Amen.**

May the love of God,
who calls us beloved children, bless you. **Amen.**

May the power of the Holy Spirit,
who descended upon Jesus as a dove,
give you peace. **Amen.**

Questions for Reflection

How may I live in the power of the Holy Spirit this day?

What in my life is like chaff that the Holy Spirit burns away in order for me
to live as a free and faithful child of God?

Household Prayer: Morning

Loving God,
we begin this new day in the sure knowledge
that you have claimed us as your children.
In all that we do,
keep us mindful of actions that are pleasing in your sight.

In all that we say,
make us attentive to the witness we give to your love.
Let our lives be an example to all whom we encounter,
living as daughters and sons of God
who follow in the path of Jesus,
our Lord and our brother. Amen.

Household Prayer: Evening

As evening comes and we end the labors of this day,
we thank you, Lord Jesus, that you have been our companion.
If we have disregarded your fellowship, forgive us.
Where we have strayed from your path, correct us.
Let us rest this evening as children of God,
sheltered in the love of those who belong to your holy family of grace.
Amen.

Second Sunday after the Epiphany

Isaiah 62:1–5   1 Corinthians 12:1–11
Psalm 36:5–10   John 2:1–11

OPENING WORDS / CALL TO WORSHIP
How precious is the steadfast love of God.   *Ps. 36:7, 9*
**All people may take refuge in the shadow of
    God's embrace.**
Christ is the fountain of life.
In Christ we behold the Light of God.

CALL TO CONFESSION
In the light of Christ,
we see the darkness of our world and of our hearts.
Trusting in God's saving love,
let us confess our sin.

PRAYER OF CONFESSION
Almighty God,   *1 Cor. 12:2*
**we confess that we have been led astray by the
    idols of our world.**
We have depended on our possessions
and have not placed our trust in your grace.
We have carelessly consumed the gifts you offer
and have failed to be faithful stewards of the earth's resources.
We have sought security in the might of the sword
rather than the strength of your Holy Spirit.
Forgive us, we pray.
Lead us to true repentance that we may serve you faithfully.
Through Christ we pray. Amen.

DECLARATION OF FORGIVENESS

Hear the good news:
Christ unmasks the idols of our world
and frees us from slavery to all that would oppress us.
In the name of Jesus Christ, we are forgiven.

PRAYER OF THE DAY

Holy God,
through signs of grace you reveal your glory to all the world.
Open our eyes to the hidden and surprising wonders you perform,
that we may believe with our minds
and trust in our hearts
that you alone are Lord of all creation.
Though Christ, in the power of the Holy Spirit, we pray. **Amen.**

PRAYER FOR ILLUMINATION

Gracious God,   *John 2:11*
by the power of the Holy Spirit,
quicken our understanding
that we may receive the testimony of Scripture
and believe in the signs that reveal your presence.
We pray in Jesus' name. **Amen.**

PRAYERS OF INTERCESSION

In peace let us pray to the Lord, saying,
    Lord, in your mercy, hear our prayer.

Loving God,
in every gathering of Christian believers,
you bring together a people of gifts, strengths, and needs
to manifest the universal body of Christ.
We pray for your church throughout the world,
that every local congregation may live as sisters and brothers
    in harmony,
showing forth the light of Christ to the world.
Lord, in your mercy, **hear our prayer**.

In every age you raise up servant leaders for your people.
We pray for all who teach and lead
[for our Bishop N., for our pastor N.],

and for all serve in the name of Christ.
Lord, in your mercy, **hear our prayer**.

For the sake of the common good of all people,
you create human societies to be places of refuge and human
    flourishing.
We pray for the leaders of the governments
and especially for our leaders
[President N., Governor N., and others in public service].
May they receive wisdom to exercise government
with true justice grounded in mercy.
Lord, in your mercy, **hear our prayer**.

Your Son, Jesus, performed the first of his signs of glory
at a wedding in Cana.
We pray for all who are joined as family:
for husbands and wives
and for all who make covenant to live together
for mutual support and love;
for parents and children,
for the aged and the young.
Lord, in your mercy, **hear our prayer**.

Lord, you are the giver of all good things:
Receive our prayers that we offer for ourselves and for our world.
In all things, grant us the courage
to exercise your gifts for the good of our world,
through Christ, in the power of the Holy Spirit. **Amen.**

INVITATION TO THE OFFERING   *Ps. 36:8, 9*

God is a generous giver of gifts
that flow like a river from the fountain of life.
Bring offerings and tributes with thanks and praise;
for the gifts we give are the gifts of God.

PRAYER OF THANKSGIVING/DEDICATION

At the wedding feast at Cana   *John 2:1–11; 1 Cor. 12:7*
you gladdened the guests with divine
    generosity,
filled to the brim and flowing over.

We offer our gifts with grateful hearts.
Bless them and our lives to your service,
that they may reveal your glory,
nurture faith, and manifest the common good.
In Jesus' name we pray. **Amen.**

CHARGE

Let us go forth rejoicing in the power of the Spirit.
Thanks be to God.

BLESSING

May the Spirit's love,   *Ps. 36:8–9; 1 Cor. 12:1–12*
flowing like water across the face of
   the earth,
fill you with every gift for the good of
   the world.
And the blessing of God,
Eternal Source, Fountain of Life, and Giver of Gifts,
be with you always. **Amen.**

Questions for Reflection

The Holy Spirit enlivens each of us with unique gifts that nurture faith
and serve the common good. To identify those gifts we can ask ourselves
such questions as, When do I feel most alive? What do I love to do? What
things, tasks, or actions fill me with a sense of purpose? What am I doing
when time seems to stand still? These questions help us discern the Spirit's
movement in our lives. Created in the image of God, each of us is uniquely
gifted to reveal divine likeness. When our deep joy is united with meaning
and purpose, vocation is birthed. How or where is God calling you?

Household Prayer: Morning

Enlivening God,   *Isa. 62:1, 4–5; Ps. 36:5, 7*
each morning I am awakened by your goodness
nudging the earth to life.
I am filled with wonder.
Your steadfast love extends to the sky,
your constancy reaches to the clouds.
How precious is your steadfast love!

It shines like the dawn,
and dews the desolation of my soul.
Manifest in me the gifts of your Spirit
that I may rejoice in you
as I delight in serving your world this day. Amen.

Household Prayer: Evening

As evening falls and darkness shutters the day,   *Isa. 62:3–4; Ps. 36:5, 7, 10*
do not forsake us, O God.
Crown the sky with jewels of light
    that your salvation may burnish the heavens
        and illumine the earth,
and all find refuge in the shadow of your wings. Amen.

Third Sunday after the Epiphany

Nehemiah 8:1–3, 5–6, 8–10   1 Corinthians 12:12–31a
Psalm 19   Luke 4:14–21

OPENING WORDS / CALL TO WORSHIP

God built the heavens, the earth, and everything in them.   *Ps. 19:1*
God calls us to be builders as well.
God calls us to build our lives:
to restore broken places and continue to grow.
God calls us to build our faith:
to study the Word and ponder its interpretation.   *Neh. 8:8*
God calls us to build our community:
to build bridges of understanding and systems of justice.
God calls us to build history by fulfilling the promises
      of Scripture:
to preach the good news of God's love and liberation
      for all people.   *Luke 4:18*

CALL TO CONFESSION

Let us confess our sin as an offering
of our trust in God's love and forgiveness for us.
[or]
In contrast to God's clear word,   *Ps. 19:12*
our faults and failings may remain hidden from others
and even from ourselves.
Confession before God can clear our eyes and cleanse our hearts,
for God's mercy is as wide as the firmament of heaven.

PRAYER OF CONFESSION

God of our Restoration,
whenever we come home to you,
we realize how far we have strayed
and how much we have forgotten

of your law and your love. *Neh. 8:9*
We have not loved you with our whole hearts
or loved our neighbors as ourselves.
Forgive us, heal us,
and restore us to our relationship with you;
through Jesus Christ, in whom we trust. Amen.

DECLARATION OF FORGIVENESS

As a called and ordained minister of Jesus Christ,
I assure you that you have been restored in the grace of God.
Do not mourn, therefore, but rejoice, *Neh. 8:10*
for this is a new day for you and for me.
[or]
God's word does not come to condemn us,
but to make us wise,
reviving our souls and rejoicing our hearts. *Ps. 19:7–8*
God's Word has been fulfilled among us in Jesus Christ,
who sets us free to live in accord with God's
own jubilee. *Luke 4:18–19, 21*

PRAYER OF THE DAY

Holy One, *Luke 4:18*
we thank you for the gift of the Bible,
for its psalms and poems, myths and stories,
histories, teachings, and prophecies.
May the Holy Spirit who called out those ancient writings
continue to call us out today,
that our lives may reflect the first sermon of Jesus,
our crucified and risen Christ,
who brings good news to the poor and lets the oppressed go free.
In Jesus' name we pray. **Amen.**

PRAYER FOR ILLUMINATION

Just as we see your wisdom and glory in nature
around us, God, *Ps. 19:1–4, 14*
may we hear your Word for us in the words of
these readings,
that by the power of the Holy Spirit we may be drawn
closer to you.
Through your great preacher, Jesus Christ, we pray. **Amen.**
[or]

We have gathered before your Word, O God.   *Neh. 8:1, 4, 8*
We want to hear with understanding, so give us
    attentive ears.
By the power of your Holy Spirit at work
in the word read and proclaimed,
make the words of our mouths   *Ps. 19:14*
and the meditations of our hearts acceptable to you,
our Rock and Redeemer. **Amen.**

PRAYERS OF INTERCESSION

God of prophets and apostles,
you call us to restore that which is broken   *Rev. 21:1*
and to proclaim your vision of a world made new.
Create in us new hearts and strong voices as we pray.   *Ps. 51:10*
God, fill us with the power of your Spirit.   *Luke 4:14*

We pray for those who have been anointed or chosen
    as leaders of people,   *Luke 4:18*
that they may attend to the voices of their people and
    be guided by you.
God, fill us with the power of your Spirit.

We pray for pastors and teachers of the church,
that they may faithfully interpret your Word for others.   *Neh. 8:8*
God, fill us with the power of your Spirit.

We pray for those who are poor and in need of assistance,
    and for ourselves,
that we may open our hearts to their cries for help.
God, fill us with the power of your Spirit.

We pray for those who are the captives of war and
    the victims of violence;   *Luke 4:18*
may we bring them good news both in word and deed.   *1 John 3:18*
God, fill us with the power of your Spirit.

We pray for those with physical challenges and
    spiritual struggles;   *Luke 4:18*
make us agents of healing and hope.
God, fill us with the power of your Spirit.

We pray for those who are oppressed by powers
    beyond their control;   *Luke 4:18*
give us courage to work to set them free.
God, fill us with the power of your Spirit.

God of the Jubilee,   *Lev. 25:10*
make us the body of the risen Christ,   *1 Cor. 12:27*
united, in all our diversity.
Animate us by your Holy Spirit   *1 Cor. 12:13*
that together we may work
toward your coming kingdom.   *Luke 11:2*
In Jesus' name we pray. **Amen.**

INVITATION TO THE OFFERING

Let us give generously from that which has been given to us,
that through our offerings
the good news of Jesus Christ may be fulfilled.   *Luke 4:21*
[or]

Each one of us is essential
to the life and well-being of the whole body of Christ.   *1 Cor. 12:14-31*
So we come now to share our gifts and resources
in order to care for one another
and, without dissension,
for the world Christ came to save.   *1 Cor. 12:25*

PRAYER OF THANKSGIVING/DEDICATION

God of life and of new life,
bless these gifts that we have given
that they may further your reign in this world.

CHARGE

Go into the world and proclaim the good news!   *Luke 4:18*
[or]

The Spirit is still at work among us,
disciples of Christ,
sending us to bring good news to the poor,
to proclaim release to those in captivity,
to be healers and a freedom force against
    all oppression,
Go boldly as disciples, trusting in the Spirit's guidance. *Luke 4:18, 17c*

BLESSING

> Go on your way, eat the fat, drink sweet wine,   *Neh. 8:10*
> and send portions of them to those who have none.
> This day is holy to our God,
> so let us all be filled with joy!

[or]

> As we go from this place on this day holy to God
> we rejoice in the strength of God,   *Neh. 8:10*
> we fix our eyes on the grace of Christ,   *Luke 4:20*
> and we drink deeply of the Spirit, who makes us one.   *1 Cor. 12:13*

Question for Reflection

The Old Testament "year of jubilee" to which Jesus refers in his first sermon—what some have called his "mission statement"—was a time set aside every fifty years to forgive financial debt and redistribute the land among the people. Why do you think God envisioned a year of jubilee, and what might that look like in our world today?

Household Prayer: Morning

Holy One, thank you for the gift of this new day.
Help me to stay attentive to your creation
and mindful of your teachings
as I travel through it.
Empower me to see and spread
the good news of your grace for all people. Amen.

Household Prayer: Evening

Holy One, thank you for the gift of today.
Thank you for all the ways that I saw your glory
and learned your teachings,
beyond speech and words,
in the course of this day.   *Ps. 19:3*
As I drift to sleep this night,
draw me closer to you,
my rock and my redeemer. Amen.   *Ps. 19:14*

Fourth Sunday after the Epiphany

Jeremiah 1:4–10   1 Corinthians 13:1–13
Psalm 71:1–6   Luke 4:21–30

OPENING WORDS / CALL TO WORSHIP
From the very beginning, God calls us.   *Jer. 1:4*
God sets us apart with a meaning and a purpose.
We come up with excuses to avoid our calls,
    for we are afraid.   *Jer. 1:6, 8*
But God reassures us in many and various ways
    through the course of our days.
Even if we are brought to the edge of a cliff,   *Luke 4:29*
God is with us and sustains us.
[or]
Our hope is in God all of our lives.   *Ps. 71:1–6*
God is a rock of refuge: a fortress against threat
    and shame.
God has held us since our birth.
So we are never in the full grasp of the unjust and cruel.
In love, God saves and supports us.
Trusting in God, we continually offer our praise!

CALL TO CONFESSION
Trust in the One who made us and redeemed us.
Let us confess our sin.
[or]
God calls us to speak the truth,
even when it is difficult,
to others but also to ourselves.
Confessing our sin in prayer,
we dare to speak the truth about ourselves to God,
who desires to deliver us and to cast out fear.   *Jer. 1:8*

PRAYER OF CONFESSION

God of life,   *1 Cor. 13:4–8*
we admit to you and to each other
that we have not always lived lives of love.
We have lost patience and been rude.
We have been irritable and insisted on our own way.
We have even let love end.
Forgive us and heal us, dear God,
through Jesus Christ, your love incarnate. Amen.

[or]

God, our Deliverer,
we confess that we are too reluctant   *Jer. 1:7*
to speak and to live according to your truth.
We grow comfortable with the way things are,
passively condoning injustice.
We see ourselves as "insiders,"
excluding those we consider "outsiders."   *Luke 4:25–27*
We find it easier to pluck up and pull down,
to destroy and overthrow,
than to build and to plant.   *Jer. 1:10*
Forgive us, O God, for being timid disciples.
Empty us of fear and shame,   *Ps. 71:1*
and fill us with love that is humble and patient
    and kind.   *1 Cor. 13:4*
We pray this in the name of the One who
    humbled himself,   *Phil. 2:8*
Jesus the Christ. Amen.

DECLARATION OF FORGIVENESS

God has loved us since the beginning,
and God's love for us will never end.
Do not fear, therefore,
but have faith in God's steadfast love,
God's healing power,
and God's ability to make all things new.

[or]

Though we know only in part, we are fully known
    to God.   *1 Cor. 13:12–13*
By the grace of Christ, God forgives us in love,
and calls us to abide in faith, in hope, and in love.

PRAYER OF THE DAY

God of life, death, and resurrection,
we are grateful for life and all its gifts.
Increase in us the stuff that life is made of—
faith, hope, and love,
but especially love—   *1 Cor. 13:13*
that we may abide with you eternally through
    Jesus Christ,
our lover and our lord. **Amen.**

PRAYER FOR ILLUMINATION

Spirit of life, God of love,
open our hearts and enter in,
that hearing your word of love,
we may become your love for others. **Amen.**

[or]

Holy Spirit,   *Jer. 1:4, 9*
as the word of the Lord came to Jeremiah in his time,
bring this word now to us.
Touch our mouths and our hearts with your word today,
that we may build on it
in our lives, in the church, and in your world. **Amen.**

PRAYERS OF INTERCESSION

God of all goodness, we live in times of stress
    and controversy,   *Ps. 71:2–6*
injustice and cruelty.
At times we cry to you for rescue
and remember that we have leaned on you since our birth
    as we pray,
O God of all creation, be our hope and trust.

We pray for leaders and nations around the world,
that they may seek justice and peace,
O God of all creation, be our hope and trust.

We pray for your church in all its forms,
that we may be the love you want,
O God of all creation, be our hope and trust.

We pray for victims of domestic violence and victims of war;
grant your healing and give your peace.
O God of all creation, be our hope and trust.

We pray for those trapped by natural disaster;
embrace them with your calm and send them relief.
O God of all creation, be our hope and trust.

We pray for those who are ill or suffering,
that they may feel the comfort of your love.
O God of all creation, be our hope and trust.

We pray for your creation,
that the health of the earth may be restored.
O God of all creation, be our hope and trust.

We pray for those who are born today and those who
will die today;
may their quality of life be governed by loving choices.
O God of all creation, be our hope and trust.

God our Wisdom, enable us to be humble and kind in all things.	*1 Cor. 13:4*
Remind us that, whatever the issue, today we know only in part.	*1 Cor. 13:9*
And even now faith, hope, and love abide; and the greatest of these is love.	*1 Cor. 13:12*
Help us to be, like you, Love;	*1 John 4:8*
through Jesus Christ, our friend and savior. **Amen.**	*John 15:15*

INVITATION TO THE OFFERING

Friends, let us love not only in our words but also in our deeds	*1 John 3:18*
through the tithes and offerings that we give today.	

PRAYER OF THANKSGIVING/DEDICATION
O God, bless these gifts that we have given
as expressions of our love
for you and our neighbors,

that they may bring closer to fulfillment
your reign of peace and love;
through Jesus Christ, our Sovereign. **Amen.**

CHARGE

Empowered by God's love for you,
go out and love your neighbors,
the ones just like you
and those different from you.   *Matt. 5:43–44*

[or]

God is a refuge, but never an escape, therefore:
Go this day into a world
where things are being pulled down and overthrown,
where things are being built and planted.   *Jer. 1:10*
Go this day open to the surprise of what God is doing
and where and with whom God is at work!   *Luke 4:25–27*
Go this day with the love of God made visible in you.   *1 Cor. 13:1–7*

BLESSING

Now may the grace of God,
the love of Christ,
and the friendship of the Holy Spirit
go with us all.

[or]

May the love of God   *1 Cor. 13:7, 13*
help you to bear all things.
May the love of Christ
enable you to believe all things.
May the love of the Holy Spirit
inspire you to hope all things,
so that you abide in faith, hope, and love
this day and forever.

Questions for Reflection

In Jesus' first sermon, he referred to two scriptural stories to illustrate God's
love. Why did that so enrage the congregation that they wanted to kill him?
Do some of Jesus' teachings still enrage us today?

Household Prayer: Morning

God, you have given me the gift of another day;
may I live it in gratitude.
Help me to be loving to others,
to Earth, and to myself;
in Jesus' name. Amen.

Household Prayer: Evening

Holy One, this day is drawing to an end.
Be with me as I pause and ponder
all the love I saw and received today.
Help me to see you in each moment of love.
Where I fell short of being patient and kind,
help me to feel your patience and kindness toward me,
and give me peace, as I give this day back to you. Amen.

Fifth Sunday after the Epiphany

Isaiah 6:1–8 (9–13)   1 Corinthians 15:1–11
Psalm 138   Luke 5:1–11

OPENING WORDS / CALL TO WORSHIP

In the sanctuary, God, the Holy One,
whose glory fills the whole earth,
calls us.   *Isa. 6:3*
Beside the sea, along ordinary paths,
in our daily work,
God calls us.   *Luke 5:1, 10*
We respond with our whole heart,
singing God's praise and giving thanks.   *Ps. 138:1–2*
In steadfast love, God fulfills
the divine purposes for our lives.   *Ps. 138:8*
[or]
We have come from different backgrounds on various
      roads to get here.
But we are all here seeking an experience of the holy.
Listen for the promise of God's steadfast love and God's
      faithfulness.   *Ps. 138:2*
We are listening for God's call in our lives.   *Isa. 6:8*

CALL TO CONFESSION

Let us turn to the most holy One and confess our sin,   *Ps. 138:2*
confident in God's faithful and steadfast love for us.

PRAYER OF CONFESSION

God of the universe and Creator of all that is,   *Isa. 6:5, 7; Luke 5:8*
we admit that we fail to be honest about our lives
      and in the politics of life.
Sometimes we are deceitful;

other times we judge ourselves harshly
and feel unworthy of your call on our lives.
Touch us with your grace
and dispel our fear,
that we may arise with renewed spirits
to serve you, our true Sovereign. Amen.
[or]

O God, though we walk in the midst of trouble,
you preserve and deliver us.   *Ps. 138:7*
Though our lips are not clean
and our hearts are not pure, you call us.   *Isa. 6:4*
Forgive us, we pray,
when we wander away from you,
lost and at risk.
Forgive us when our lives do not reflect your glory
and the purposes you intend.
Help us to comprehend your ways in the world.   *Isa. 6:9–10*
We long to feel your grace and glory,   *Isa. 6:1*
for in you, Emmanuel, we can be healed and set free;   *Matt. 9:21*
in Jesus' name, we pray. Amen.

DECLARATION OF FORGIVENESS

The promise is this:
God is faithful and steadfast,
eager to forgive our sin and welcome us home.
Grateful for this promise of joy and of peace,
let us share the peace of Christ with one another.
[or]

In the temple, Isaiah heard these words:
"Your guilt has departed and your sin is blotted out."   *Isa. 6:7*
God's grace toward us has not been in vain!
This is the good news we have received:
in Christ's death and resurrection,
we have been saved.   *1 Cor. 15:10, 2–4*
Thanks be to God!

PRAYER OF THE DAY

Holy One,   *Isa. 6:3*
earth and heaven reverberate with your glory,
and humans and angels alike sing your praises.

Open our minds to your breathtaking work in the world,
even as you call us
to spread the good news of Jesus Christ, our mentor and savior,
in whose name we pray. **Amen.**

PRAYER FOR ILLUMINATION

God of Exodus and Resurrection,   *1 Cor. 15:1, 3*
we are grateful for the gift of Scripture.
By the power of the Holy Spirit,
enliven your Word,
that we might know the good news
and share it with others.
For the sake of Christ we ask it. **Amen.**

[or]

God of steadfast love and faithfulness,
you have exalted your name and your word above everything.
By the power of your Holy Spirit,
help us to hear your word with understanding,
that in our speech and actions,
we may exalt your name above all things;
in Jesus' name we ask it. **Amen.**

PRAYERS OF INTERCESSION

O God most high, you meet us where we live
and invite us to be part of your purpose.
All thanks and praise to you,
for you hear our prayers
for the church, the world, and all who live in it.
On the day I called, you answered me;   *Ps. 138:3*
you increased my strength of soul.

We pray for the church
and for all who work to bring others a word of compassion.
On the day I called, you answered me;
you increased my strength of soul.

We pray for peace among nations and peace among people.
On the day I called, you answered me;
you increased my strength of soul.

We pray for those suffering from war or calamities of nature.
On the day I called, you answered me;
you increased my strength of soul.

We pray for those who are oppressed and need courage to resist.
On the day I called, you answered me;
you increased my strength of soul.

We pray for those who because of illness or hardship
are paralyzed by fear.
On the day I called, you answered me;
you increased my strength of soul.

God of majesty and glory,
through Jesus Christ you summon us
into your compassion for all creation.
Renew in us your call and release us from all fear,
that we may testify in words and deeds
to your steadfast love for all.
For the sake of Jesus Christ we pray. **Amen.**

INVITATION TO THE OFFERING

Through Jesus Christ we have come to know the
abundance of God.   *Luke 5:6*
Let us then give generously, as has been given to us.
[or]
We are invited to cast our nets into God's abundance,   *Luke 5:4, 7*
and to share what we have received with others.
As we give our tithes and offerings today,
we put our trust in the one who has called us to follow him:
Jesus Christ, the great Fisher of people.

PRAYER OF THANKSGIVING/DEDICATION

Holy One, we give you thanks
for your generosity to us.
Bless these gifts and multiply them,
for the sake of those in need around us;
in Jesus' name. **Amen.**

CHARGE

Don't be afraid! *Luke 5:10*
Go and be fishers of people.

[or]

Don't be afraid to put out into the deep water; *Luke 5:4, 7*
we are not alone.
We have partners in other boats beside us,
and Christ has gone before us.
Let down your nets,
expecting God's abundant provision.

BLESSING

Now may we be filled with the love of God *Ps. 138:1, 8; Luke 5:10*
and sing praises with our whole hearts,
giving thanks for the call of Christ in our lives
and the community of the Holy Spirit,
the fulfillment of the purpose for which we were created.

[or]

May the Holy One fill you with awe; *Ps. 138:3*
May Christ, the Teacher, amaze you with grace;
And may the Holy Spirit increase your strength of soul.

Questions for Reflection

Sometimes we are afraid to tell others about our experiences of the
holy and about God's call in our lives, because we don't want to annoy
or oppress others. There is a difference between witnessing through
indoctrination and witnessing through acts of compassion. How do you
witness to others about your faith?

The disciples had already fished all night without catching anything;
what quality or characteristic in Peter might have helped him "give it
another try" when Jesus invited him to cast his net again? What quality
or characteristic within you helps you to keep trying, to start again, after
disappointment or even failure?

Household Prayer: Morning

God, I give you thanks this morning *Isa. 6:3, 8; Ps. 138:3*
as I watch the beauty of the newborn light,

listen to the first stirrings of a new day in nature,
and ponder the miracle of my own breathing
and your presence in it all.
Holy, Holy, Holy!
Increase my strength of soul today.
And whenever I see a need,
help me to respond, "Send me!" Amen.

Household Prayer: Evening

Thank you, God, for the gift of this day.   *Luke 5:8, 10*
Like the fisher folk who became disciples,
I have put in a day of work.
As evening comes, it is time to rest.
If, as I review my day, I am tempted to say,
"I am not worthy of your presence, God,"
reassure me with the calming words of Jesus,
"Do not be afraid, come be with me." Amen.

Sixth Sunday after the Epiphany

Jeremiah 17:5–10   1 Corinthians 15:12–20
Psalm 1   Luke 6:17–26

OPENING WORDS / CALL TO WORSHIP

Blessed are those who trust in the Lord.   *Jer. 17:7-8*
They shall be like a tree planted by water,
sending out its roots by the stream.
Baptized and freed,
grounded in love,
let us worship God.

[or]

When we turn our hearts away from God and toward
    ourselves,   *Jer.17:5–8*
putting trust in our own strength,
we become like a shrub in the desert,
living in a parched, salty place.
When we trust in God, when our trust *is* God,
we are like a tree planted by water.
Our roots go deep, we are ever-green;
even in a drought we are not anxious,
but bear fruit, full and beautiful,
gifts of the God who made us.

CALL TO CONFESSION

If we say we have no sin, we deceive ourselves   *1 John 1:8; Jer. 17:7*
and the truth is not in us.
So let us be honest and confess what separates us
from God and our neighbors,
    trusting in God's constant desire to forgive and renew.

[or]

The prophet Jeremiah says that God tests
    our minds   *Jer. 17:10; Ps. 139:23–24*
and searches our hearts,
because the condition of mind and heart affects actions.
Trusting in God's mercy, let us invite God to search us,
so that God might also lead us in the way everlasting.

PRAYER OF CONFESSION

God of judgment and renewal,
we admit to you and to each other
that we have not always loved you and our neighbors
as fully as you call us to love.
We have failed to be good stewards
of the air, the water, the animals, and the plants.
We have turned away from you
and toward our own self-interest.
We have been shortsighted,
and we are humbly sorry.
Help us turn back to you, O Lord,
to reach toward you as a tree sends its roots out
    toward water. Amen.   *Jer. 17:8*

[or]

Merciful God, your call to discipleship is
    demanding.   *Luke 6:20–22*
You call us to reorder our lives
by the kingdom you are bringing in Jesus Christ.
Yet we still pass by the ones you especially notice:
people who are poor and hungry;
people who weep.
We have not stood with those
who are hated, bullied, and excluded.
Comfortable with the way things are,
we are too complacent,
even complicit with injustice and prejudice.
Forgive us, O God,
and turn us back to your gospel.
We pray this now, for our sake,
and for the sake of your world;
through Jesus Christ our Lord. Amen.

DECLARATION OF FORGIVENESS

Because Christ has been raised from the dead, *1 Cor. 15:14, 17*
sin and death do not have the last word!
Our faith is not in vain!
Baptized into Christ's death and resurrection,
we are forgiven and set free to live for God and neighbor.
Thanks be to God.

PRAYER OF THE DAY

God of life, in Christ you resurrect all things. *1 Cor. 15:20, 22*
Raise us from death to life,
that our transformation may bear witness
to the power of your grace in our lives
through Jesus Christ, the firstborn from the dead. *Col. 1:18*
Amen.

[or]

God our Delight, *Ps. 1:1–2*
your word guides us in paths that are true.
We do not want to walk so long in sin
that we take our place among those opposed to your ways,
or settle down in the company of ridicule.
Watch over us, we pray,
as we meditate on you day and night,
and we will be happy. **Amen.**

PRAYER FOR ILLUMINATION

Creator God, you created us with free will
and freedom of choice.
By the power of the Holy Spirit,
speak your Word though the words of scripture,
that we may live according to your will;
through Jesus Christ, in whose name we pray. **Amen.**

[or]

O God, *Jer. 17:8, 10c; Luke 6:25*
whose Word is like water to the root
 of the tree,
let your Word now flow into us
that we might flourish—
bearing gospel fruit for a hungry world.
In the name of Jesus, the Living Word, we pray. **Amen.**

PRAYERS OF INTERCESSION

Holy One, you have created us with the ability
to choose
between life and death, blessings and curses.
Help us to reject the advice of the wicked or sit with the scoffers,
and by your grace, empower us to put our trust in you.
Blessed are those who trust in the Lord, whose trust is the Lord.

*Luke 6:17–26;
Ps. 1:1; Jer. 17:5, 7*

We pray for those who put their trust in themselves instead of in you.
Blessed are those who trust in the Lord, whose trust is the Lord.

We pray for those who put their trust in princes and politicians,
and find themselves deceived and misled.
Blessed are those who trust in the Lord, whose trust is the Lord.

We pray for those who are poor, who hunger, who weep.
Blessed are those who trust in the Lord, whose trust is the Lord.

We pray for those who are making poor choices in their lives;
may they turn to you for guidance.
Blessed are those who trust in the Lord, whose trust is the Lord.

We pray for the trees, for the rivers and streams, and for all your
creation:
turn us from our exploitative ways to help you renew the earth.
Blessed are those who trust in the Lord, whose trust is the Lord.

God, you demand much, but promise that your yoke is easy.
Guide us throughout our lives,
keeping us ever mindful of the good news
of your forgiving and renewing grace;
through Jesus Christ, our Lord. **Amen.**

INVITATION TO THE OFFERING

God places before us
the ways of life and the ways of death
and bids us to choose.
As we prepare to give our tithes and offerings this day,
let us choose wisely,
guided by the Holy Spirit who dwells among us.
[or]

Deut. 30:19

Luke tells us that people came to Jesus from all
 directions,   Luke 6:17–18, 20
seeking healing and peace.
We are the body of Christ,
surrounded by the many needs of the world around us.
So bring your tithes and offerings,
that these gifts may foster healing and encourage peace.

PRAYER OF THANKSGIVING/DEDICATION

Holy One, bless and multiply these gifts we give   *Jer. 17:7-8; Luke 6:20*
as tokens of our trust in you.
Use them to bless the poor,
feed the hungry, and comfort those who weep;
in Jesus' name. **Amen.**

CHARGE

Hear the word of our Lord, Jesus Christ: *Luke 6:22*
When people hate you, exclude you, revile you,
 defame you,
do not dismay,
for that is also how they treated the prophets before you!
[or]
Consider this day
the ways in which you are falsely consoled
and uncomfortably full.
Consider today how casual attitudes
turn us aside from tears too deep for words.
Consider this day the kingdom
and the strange blessing it promises.

BLESSING

May you be like trees planted by water   *Jer. 17:8; Ps. 1:1, 6*
who yield your fruit in its season,
watched over and protected by God.
[or]
May the blessing of God,   *Jer. 17:8; Luke 6:20–26;*
Creator, Christ, and Holy Spirit,   *1 Cor. 15:17–19*
nourish and sustain us,
surprise and reorder us,
and strengthen us in faith and hope for this life and the life to come.

Questions for Reflection

One commentator on Luke 6:17–26 writes, "'Blessed' (*makarios*) does not simply describe a state of happiness or bliss. Rather, it refers in a theological sense to one's standing before God (Deut. 33:29; Pss. 1:1; 40:4)."* As you reflect on the blessings and woes in Luke's Gospel and on the use of the word "happy" in Psalm 1:1 and "blessed" in Jeremiah 17:7, how does this meaning of "blessed" or "happy" contrast with contemporary uses of this word, even by some preachers? What is one change you can make in your own life before God that would bring you into closer accord with Jesus' understanding of blessedness?

Household Prayer: Morning

Gracious God, thank you for the gift of this new day.   Ps. 119:133
Guide my steps as I face choices to care for the earth or not,
to show compassion toward others or not, to care for myself or not,
to be true to Christ or not.
May each of my choices draw me closer to you. Amen.

Household Prayer: Evening

Tonight I come home to you in prayer, my God.
Thank you for guiding me through this day,
even when I was not conscious of it.
Now I give this day back to you,
entrusting all that I did and all that I left undone
to your compassionate care.
May I rest in peace. Amen.

*From Gay L. Byron, "Exegetical Perspective" on Luke 6:17–26, Sixth Sunday after the Epiphany, in *Feasting on the Word: Preaching the Revised Common Lectionary, Year C, Volume 4*, ed. David L. Bartlett and Barbara Brown Taylor (Louisville, KY: Westminster John Knox Press, 2009), 361.

Seventh Sunday after the Epiphany

Genesis 45:3–11, 15   1 Corinthians 15:35–38, 42–50
Psalm 37:1–11, 39–40   Luke 6:27–38

OPENING WORDS / CALL TO WORSHIP

Take delight in the Lord,   *Ps. 37:4–5, 7, 39*
who satisfies the desires of your heart.
Commit your way to the Lord
and trust in God's actions.
Be still before the Lord
and wait patiently for God.
The Lord is our salvation
and our refuge in times of trouble.
[or]

How can the dead be raised to life?   *1 Cor. 15:35–36, 50; John 12:24*
The single grain of wheat that falls to
    the earth will die—
but when it does, it will come to life again
and bear much good fruit for the kingdom
    of God.

CALL TO CONFESSION

[At the font, pouring water]
Jesus promised us that God is kind   *Luke 6:35*
even to the ungrateful and the wicked,
even to us.
Trusting in God's kindness and love,
let us confess our sin.

PRAYER OF CONFESSION

Merciful God, we confess
that we have not followed your ways

78

or trusted your promises.
We love only those who love us;
we show kindness only to those who are kind to us;
we give only when we expect to receive.
Forgive us, Lord.
Fill our hearts with your selfless love.
Change our lives by your matchless grace.
These things we pray through Christ our Savior. Amen.

DECLARATION OF FORGIVENESS

[At the font, lifting water]
Children of the Most High God,   *Luke 6:35–39*
through Jesus Christ our Lord
we have received grace in good measure—
spilling out and running over.
Thanks be to God.

Now go and live as Christ commands:
Be merciful, as God is merciful;
do not judge, and you will not be judged;
do not condemn, and you will not be condemned;
but forgive, and you will be forgiven;
give, and it will be given to you. **Amen.**

PRAYER OF THE DAY

God of abundant mercy,
you alone can turn evil into good,
sorrow into rejoicing,
and death into everlasting life.
Teach us your way of grace—
to meet hatred with kindness,
to answer curses with blessing,
to love without holding back,
to give without thought of return;
all in the name of Jesus Christ our Lord. **Amen.**

PRAYER FOR ILLUMINATION

Gracious God, by your Word   *Gen. 45:3–11, 15*
you provide all we need—
for salvation,

for wholeness,
for abundant life.
Now draw us close in your Spirit
so that we may discover your will
and live according to your purposes;
through Jesus Christ our Lord. **Amen.**

PRAYERS OF INTERCESSION

Let us offer our intercessions to God, saying,
God in your mercy, hear our prayer.

Holy God, your cross stands before us as a light
that shows us our failures and our salvation through your Son.
We thank you for forgiving us
and for coming among us to heal our pain and resentments.
We yearn for your word and praise you for your love.
God, in your mercy, **hear our prayer.**

You who preserves life,
who sends among your people caretakers and peacemakers,
who gives us scientists and inventors,
give your people new eyes to behold the needs of your creation.
Lead us into fields of wheat and pools of clean water.
Shelter the earth with clouds; nurture the soil with sun.
Make our gratitude so profound that with joy
we will love and guard what you have created for our very lives.
God, in your mercy, **hear our prayer.**

O Giver of prayer that groans within us,
teach us to pray for our enemies.
Their names are many,
and we whisper some of them now before you in our hearts . . .
[keep silence for a time]
Be with them, guard them from harm,
and guide them in the way of your light.
Save us from self-righteousness,
and help us begin our lives anew,
God, in your mercy, **hear our prayer.**

Heal the nations, Mighty Lord.
Rain peace on all people.
Give hope to the hopeless and love to the lonely.
Surprise the leaders of all nations with your joy.
For the people . . . *[name nations in turmoil or need in the present time]*,
we cry out for reconciliation and plenty.
God, in your mercy, **hear our prayer**.

We beg comfort for the sick, O God.
Make whole the broken,
make wise the foolish,
humble the powerful,
make glad the hearts of those who tend our loved ones,
and for any who are in pain,
give them release and rest.
Speak love to . . . *[name those who have asked for prayer]*
and to all who cry out silently.
God, in your mercy, **hear our prayer**.

Now hear, O God, the prayers of this assembly
spoken silently or aloud . . . *[silence for people to name petitions]*.
God, in your mercy, **hear our prayer**.

Savior of the world,
we give you thanks for the church,
for the meek, for the courageous,
for those who teach us how to wait.
We praise you for the life-giving spirit
that inhabits the saints whose visions have shown the path.
We thank you for . . . *[name any of the church's saints whose
    commemorations fall in the coming week]* and for the biblical witness
    of Joseph and his brothers
in stories rich enough to feed us, along with them, with your mercy.
Make us truly grateful for prophets and dreamers.
God, in your mercy, **hear our prayer**.

Trusting in the mercy of your never-failing wisdom,
we commend into your hands all for whom we pray;
through Jesus Christ, our Savior and Lord. **Amen.**

INVITATION TO THE OFFERING

Children of the Most High God,
in obedience to Jesus' words to love others as we love ourselves,
do good, bless and pray for friends and enemies alike,
let us now do to others as we would have them do to us,
offering our tithes and gifts
for the sake of our sisters and brothers in need.

PRAYER OF THANKSGIVING/DEDICATION

Holy God, you have given us land in which to grow and thrive,
food for survival and pleasure,
air and water, fire and cold.
Make our thanksgiving bloom forth into the lives of others
in the name of the one who gave everything for us. **Amen.**

CHARGE

Do not judge, and you will not be judged;   *Luke 6:37–38*
do not condemn, and you will not be condemned.
Forgive, and you will be forgiven;
give, and it will be given to you.
For God is kind to all and full of mercy.
Filled with life-giving spirit of our Creator, Redeemer,
    and Sustainer,
we bear the image of the risen one
and take delight in the abundance of what we have
    already received.

BLESSING

Now may the Lord who sent Joseph to Egypt
and gave him tears of joy at reunion with his family,
surround your days with strong visions,
worthy work, reconciliations,
and the strength to persevere,
in the name of the Father, Son, and Holy Spirit,
One God, Mother of us all.

Questions for Reflection

How has God sent you to be a preserver of what is good and healthy?

How is your family living up to the wisdom that Joseph showed in caring for the people of Egypt and, eventually, even his own kin?

Household Prayer: Morning

In the morning when I rise, O God,
you are with me strong and sure,
turning my dreams into insights
and teaching me the delights of your law.
You preserve my life day after day,
and in return, I rejoice at the new dawn.
Guard my waiting this day, O Lord,
guide my feet and my hands,
give me stillness and patience
so that I may give delight to myself
and to those I meet;
in Jesus' name I pray. Amen.

Household Prayer: Evening

Lord, throughout this day you have rescued us from harm and despair,
giving us instead the joy of accomplishment
and fellowship with our family and friends.
Protect us through the night, Holy One,
that in our dreams we will not be shaken
but will see you face to face and wake renewed.
We take refuge in you; in Jesus' name. Amen.

Eighth Sunday after the Epiphany

Isaiah 55:10–13   1 Corinthians 15:51–58
Psalm 92:1–4, 12–15   Luke 6:39–49

OPENING WORDS / CALL TO WORSHIP

It is good to give thanks to you, O Lord,   *Ps. 92:1–2, 4*
to sing praises to you, O God Most High,
to declare your steadfast love in the morning
and your faithfulness by night.
For you, O Lord, have made me glad by your work;
at the work of your hands I sing for joy.

[or]

Listen, says the apostle Paul: *1 Cor. 15:51–52, 57*
I will tell you a mystery!
We will not all die, but we will be changed;
in a moment, in the twinkling of an eye, at the last trumpet,
the dead will be raised to life.
Thanks be to God, who gives us the victory
through our Lord Jesus Christ.

CALL TO CONFESSION

[From the font, pouring water]
When the flood surges and the river rises,   *Luke 6:48–49*
be thankful that your house is established
on the rock of God's unfailing love.
Trusting in the Lord, let us confess our sin.

PRAYER OF CONFESSION

Loving God, we confess
that our lives are choked and tangled in sin.
We call you Lord,   *Luke 6:39–49*
but we do not live according to your word.

We are quick to point out others' faults,
but oblivious to our own.
We treasure what is evil
and squander your good gifts.
Forgive us, we pray.
Redeem us, restore us,
recreate us by your grace;
through Jesus Christ our Savior. Amen.

DECLARATION OF FORGIVENESS

[From the font, lifting water]
Where, O death, is your victory?   *1 Cor. 15:51–58*
Where, O death, is your sting?
The sting of death is sin—
but God has swallowed up death forever,
and sin has no more power over us.
In Jesus Christ, we are forgiven!
Thanks be to God.

Therefore, beloved, be steadfast, be faithful,
excelling in the work of the Lord;
in the Lord, your labor will not be in vain. **Amen.**

PRAYER OF THE DAY

Holy One, our rock, our redeemer,   *Ps. 92:12–15; Luke 6:48–49*
your righteousness is unshakable;
your faithfulness is sure.
Establish us on the foundation of your Word,
so that we may stand firm in faith
and be steadfast in your service;
through Jesus Christ our Lord. **Amen.**

PRAYER FOR ILLUMINATION

Lord God, the Word that goes forth from your mouth   *Isa. 55:10–13*
does not return empty,
but accomplishes that which you intend.
Now plant your Word within us
and pour out your Spirit upon us
so that we may bear good fruit;
for the sake of Jesus Christ our Lord. **Amen.**

PRAYERS OF INTERCESSION

Let us pray for the church, the world,
and all those who are in need of prayer, saying,
   In your great mercy, hear our prayer.

O Word of life,
who by your speaking made all existence come into being,
you lead us out in joy and back in peace;
you fill the mountains and meadows with song;
through your power we are made whole.
   In your great mercy, **hear our prayer.**

O God who makes glad the trees,
we give you thanks for all your plants,
the fruits and vegetables you have made to grow;
for all manner of creatures;
for your good water and air.
Gladden the hearts of all people so that out of gratitude,
we will together care for Earth, our home, with wisdom.
   In your great mercy, **hear our prayer.**

God of justice,
you who gives tradition and renewal,
stability and change,
bedrock and shifting sands,
we pray for the nations of the world,
for presidents, prime ministers, dictators, and governors;
for civil servants, judges, parliaments, and protesters;
for people who work for peace and those who imprison;
for those whose struggles we cannot see
and those whose struggles are ours.
   In your great mercy, **hear our prayer.**

God of our weary years,
we pray for the elderly and those who are nearing death this day;
for children who are hungry and frightened;
for refugees and people whose homes are washed away in floods;
for those who have demeaning work,
those who have no work,
and all people who work in physical pain.

We pray for those we name now silently or aloud *[allow a time of silence]*.
Guide and move your people so that we may know our labors
are not in vain.
In your great mercy, **hear our prayer.**

Ancient of Days, you know the wisdom of the ancestors
on whose faith we stand,
especially *[. . . insert names of those to be remembered: the saints
whose commemoration day falls in the coming week and those in
the congregation who have died in the past week.]*.
For all the good fruit your people have borne, we give you thanks.
Make us worthy of their lives and trusting in your promises.
In your great mercy, **hear our prayer.**

We commend to you all those for whom we pray,
clinging to your promises,
through Jesus Christ, our Lord. **Amen.**

INVITATION TO THE OFFERING
Hearing the Word of the Lord,
let us respond with our tithes and offerings.

PRAYER OF THANKSGIVING/DEDICATION
Holy One, all that we have comes from you.
You bless our lives with the joy of thanksgiving
and shower upon us the help we need every hour.
Lead us, guide us;
use us and these gifts
for the sake of the life of the world,
in the name of the One who died and rose. **Amen.**

CHARGE
Go out in joy, giving thanks for God's victory over death,
for the home you have in Christ Jesus, the solid rock,
and for the Word of God that sustains all things
in faith and hope.
Remembering the log in your vision,
live with compassion for others.
Rejoice and give thanks always.

BLESSING

You do not walk alone.
The Lord God rains down upon you blessings,
power, wisdom, understanding, and mercy.

Question for Reflection

If I cannot see the log in my vision, how can I remind myself that it exists?

Household Prayer: Morning

God of waking and sleeping,
we give you thanks that you have brought the morning
and opened our minds to a new day.
Give us courage for the events that will unfold in the next hours.
Help us to see our neighbors as you see them.
Show us the way of peace. Amen.

Household Prayer: Evening

God of all compassion, our rock and our salvation,
for all that we have done today that bears good fruit,
we give you thanks.
For all that we have done today that has missed your purposes,
we ask forgiveness.
Restore us to your strong foundation,
and assure us of your love.
Protect us now in sleep from all danger.
This we pray in Jesus' name. Amen.

Ninth Sunday after the Epiphany

1 Kings 8:22–23,41–43   Galatians 1:1–12
Psalm 96:1–9   Luke 7:1–10

OPENING WORDS / CALL TO WORSHIP

Come, all of you, into the presence of the Lord   *Luke 7:10; Gal. 1:11*
where the word of God speaks peace
to those who are worthy
and those who think they are not.
Come, hear the word of the Lord,
who opens to everyone wisdom and life,
a gospel not proclaimed from human origin
but from the heart of Christ, our healer and redeemer.

CALL TO CONFESSION

Do not desert the One who calls you
in the grace of Christ,   *Gal. 1:6; Ps. 96:9*
but tremble before God's holy splendor,
speaking your confession with humility and trust.

PRAYER OF CONFESSION

Merciful God,
our fault is always before you
and our lack of faith apparent.
We confess that we have not loved our neighbors as ourselves,
we have not done the things that we intend to do,
and we have not loved you.
We have squandered time and purpose.
Give us new life, renew our direction, heal our broken
intentions.
Forgive us, through Jesus Christ our Savior. Amen.

DECLARATION OF FORGIVENESS

The Lord our God keeps covenant with all who cry out for mercy.
Through Christ Jesus and in communion with the whole church
answering repentance with absolution,
I now say to you what God has proclaimed:
In the name of Jesus, your sins are forgiven.

PRAYER OF THE DAY

Holy and life-giving God,
who hears the prayers of those in distress
and of those who sing for joy,
we give you thanks for the ever-enlarging fellowship of your people,
for your steadfast love for all creation,
and for the many ways your healing comes to us;
in Jesus' name. **Amen.**

PRAYER FOR ILLUMINATION

Open our ears, O God,
that by the power of the Holy Spirit
your mercy may dwell in our hearts
toward all your people.
Let your love for all creation
come even to us in this hour;
through Jesus Christ we pray. **Amen.**

PRAYERS OF INTERCESSION

[Possible response to each petition:]
Only say the word, Lord,   *Luke 7:7*
and all shall be well.

Lord God, there is no one like you   *1 Kgs. 8:23*
in heaven above or on the earth below.
Hear our prayers:

For your church in every place,
make us servants of Christ and witnesses to the gospel.

For leaders and people in every land,   *1 Kgs. 8 :43*
that they may know your way and do your will.

For the earth that you have made,	*Ps. 96:11-12*
that it may flourish in beauty and show your glory.	

For those who are ill and close to death,   *Luke 7:2*
draw near to them with life-giving power.

Receive all these prayers   *1 Kgs. 8:42*
in the tenderness of your mighty hand
and keep us forever
in the safety of your outstretched arm;
through Christ our Lord we pray. **Amen.**

INVITATION TO THE OFFERING

Honor and majesty belong to the Lord;   *Ps. 96:6, 8*
strength and beauty are in God's sanctuary.
Ascribe to the Lord the glory that is due;
come into God's presence
with an offering of thankfulness and praise.

PRAYER OF THANKSGIVING/DEDICATION

O Lord, you are great and greatly to be praised.   *Ps. 96:4*
Receive these gifts of gratitude and joy
and use them in the service of the gospel
and for the glory of your holy name. **Amen.**

CHARGE AND BLESSING

Walk before God in faithfulness   *1 Kgs. 8:23*
and humbleness of heart,
and may the Lord God, in steadfast love,
keep covenant with you forever.

Question for Reflection

The centurion in Luke 7:1–10, who described himself as "a man set under authority," trusted the authority of God in Jesus Christ. He was confident that if Jesus would "only speak the word" his servant would be healed. In our age of broken trust and questionable authority, it is difficult to have such confidence in earthly leaders. But do we have that kind of faith in God?

Household Prayer: Morning

Lord Jesus Christ,
in the uncertainty and anxiety of the day before us
help us to trust your word
and believe in your promises,
so that we may be messengers
of your good news and healing love;
in your holy name we pray. Amen.

Household Prayer: Evening

Lord Jesus Christ,
as darkness draws near,
come to us and make us whole.
Remain with us this night
and bless and keep us all our days;
in your holy name we pray. Amen.

Transfiguration Sunday
(Last Sunday before Lent)

Exodus 34:29–35   2 Corinthians 3:12–4:2
Psalm 99   Luke 9:28–36 (37–43)

OPENING WORDS / CALL TO WORSHIP

"The LORD is king;   *Ps. 99:1–2, 9*
let the people tremble."
The Lord is enthroned upon the cherubim;
let the earth shake. . . .
Proclaim the greatness of the Lord
and worship upon God's holy hill;
for the Lord our God is the Holy One.
[or]
All of us, with unveiled faces   *2 Cor. 3:18*
are being transformed
from one degree of glory to another;
this comes from the Lord, the Spirit.

CALL TO CONFESSION

In trust, let us call upon God's holy name,
confess our sin, and receive forgiveness.

PRAYER OF CONFESSION

Merciful and gracious God,
we bow before your unending compassion,
the measure of our falling short.
We have not loved as you command.
We have not spoken truly.
We have not cared for creation, including ourselves,
according to your will.
What we intend, we have not pursued;
what we mean to avoid, we embrace.

Help us to know the mind of Christ,
that in all thoughts, words, and deeds,
our lives might come to honor you. Amen.

DECLARATION OF FORGIVENESS

When one turns to the Lord, the veil is removed. *2 Cor. 3:16*
As a called and ordained minister of the church of Christ,
and by the authority of the Holy Spirit
working among God's holy people,
I declare your sins forgiven.
Turn now with unveiled faces,
and see to the health of all creation as newborn children of God.

PRAYER OF THE DAY

Holy God, present in our midst yet beyond all comprehension,
by your light, we see light;
by your healing, we are made whole;
by your mercy, we know your greatness.
Turn your gaze upon our weakness and show us the way of your love
that we may live with unveiled faces,
through Jesus Christ, who lives and reigns with you and the Holy Spirit,
one God, now and forever. **Amen.**

PRAYER FOR ILLUMINATION

By your Spirit, O God,
enlighten our hearts, open our minds,
fill our vision with your radiance,
and give us life,
as we hear your Word today. **Amen.**

PRAYERS OF INTERCESSION

[A period of silence may follow each intercession.]
[Possible response to each intercession:]
To you, O Lord, we pray.
Answer us with mercy. *Ps. 99:8; 2 Cor. 4:1*

Almighty, all-merciful God,
lover of justice and giver of peace,
Hear our prayer:

For your people Israel,
for the church of Jesus Christ,
and for all who seek your face.

For leaders and elders
that they will abide by your commandments.

For the earth that you have made,   *Ps. 99:1*
trembling for redemption and re-creation.

For those who are tormented
by the demons of illness, addiction, and grief.

Let our lives and our world
be transfigured by your glory
and transformed by your love;
in the name of Jesus Christ,
your chosen one, our Lord. **Amen.**

INVITATION TO THE OFFERING

We serve the Lord with freedom;
we worship God with joy.
In freedom and in joy,
let us present the offerings of our lives to the Lord.

PRAYER OF THANKSGIVING/DEDICATION

Holy are you, O Lord!   *Ps. 99:3*
We praise your great and awesome name.
Use us, and these our gifts, in your service,
to establish justice, righteousness, and equity,
all for the good of your people
and the glory of your eternal realm. **Amen.**

CHARGE

Since we have such hope,   *2 Cor. 3:12, 17*
live and act with boldness!
Love and serve the Lord
in the freedom of the Spirit.

BLESSING

> May the glory of the Lord shine upon you,
> the Word of the Lord live within you,
> and the Spirit of the Lord give you peace.

Questions for Reflection

Look at Luke 9:35: "This is my Son, my Chosen; listen to him!" Where have you heard words like these before in the Gospels? (Hint: see Luke 3:22.) Where have you heard words like these in your own life? When have you had a strong sense of being chosen, claimed, and called by God? How have you responded?

Household Prayer: Morning

Lord Jesus Christ, as morning dawns,
be our light in this new day.
Let our lives reflect your glory,
our words show forth your goodness,
and our actions shine with your grace;
in your holy name we pray. Amen.

Household Prayer: Evening

Lord Jesus Christ, as evening comes,
be our light and hope in darkness.
Draw near to us in grace,
surround us with your presence,
and fill us with your peace;
in your holy name we pray. Amen.

Ash Wednesday

Isaiah 58:1–12   2 Corinthians 5:20b–6:10
Psalm 51:1–17   Matthew 6:1–6, 16–21

OPENING WORDS / CALL TO WORSHIP
Grace and peace in Jesus Christ our Lord.
Amen.
The Lord will guide you continually
and satisfy your needs in parched places.   *Isa. 58:11*
Thanks be to God.

CALL TO CONFESSION
Trusting in divine mercy,
and with humble hearts,
let us confess our sins before God and one another.

PRAYER OF CONFESSION
Merciful God, whose ways are good and true,
we confess that we have not lived as Christ has called us to live.
We have shut our eyes to evils our world allows.
We have sealed our ears from the cries of the suffering whose
     pain we abide.
We have clung to the hostility we harbor against one another
and hardened our hearts to the creative power of love.

Therefore we pray:
Open our eyes to see injustice in our world.   *Isa. 58:1–12*
**Give us courage to resist the powers that oppress
     the poor.**
Open our ears to hear the cry of the needy.
**Teach us generosity for sharing the abundance of
     your creation.**

Open our minds to imagine an end to human strife.
Grant us wisdom to pursue the ways of peace.
Open our hearts to love our neighbors and our enemies
  near and far.
Give us desire to embody the compassion of Christ.
For the sake of the world, in the name of Christ we pray.
Amen.

DECLARATION OF FORGIVENESS

According to the Lord's abundant mercy,   *Ps. 51:1*
there is forgiveness for all who seek repentance,
and grace for all who turn their hearts to the way of Jesus.
Thanks be to God.

PRAYER OF THE DAY

Almighty God,   *Ps. 51:12*
through love you have made us,
and for love you call us to repentance.
Grant that we who seek to mend our sinful ways
may find strength in your compassion and forgiveness.
Restore to us the joy of your salvation;
give us your Holy Spirit that we may serve you with
  willing hearts,
bearing witness to your abundant mercy in all the world;
through Christ our Lord,
who lives and reigns with you and the Holy Spirit,
one God, forever and ever. **Amen.**

PRAYER FOR ILLUMINATION

O Lord, by your Spirit   *Isa. 58:11*
open to us the Words of Life,
a spring of water that shall never fail. **Amen.**

PRAYERS OF INTERCESSION

In peace let us pray to the Lord, saying,
  Lord have mercy.

For the church throughout the world,
that all who bear the name of Christ
may find true repentance for their sins

and walk in the ways of the peace,
let us pray to the Lord.
Lord, have mercy.

For the nations of the world,
wherever there is poverty, war, or oppression of human spirit,
that all people may repent of the evil they do to one another,
let us pray to the Lord.
Lord, have mercy.

For the planet Earth, God's gift to humankind,
that we repent of selfish or thoughtless exploitation
and tend it with care so that all may share justly in its bounty,
let us pray to the Lord.
Lord, have mercy.

For the leaders of the nations,
that they may work for the common good of all people
and repent of arrogant nationalism,
let us pray to the Lord.
Lord, have mercy.

For our enemies,
that we may learn to love them with regard for God's compassion,
forgiving wrongs and seeking reconciliation,
let us pray to the Lord.
Lord, have mercy.

For those who are sick or in trouble,
for the defenseless, the weak, and the poor,
that they may find help in time of need,
and that the church may heed their cry,
let us pray to the Lord.
Lord, have mercy.

Loving God,
hear the prayers of your people for the sake of our world.
With our prayers, accept the dedication of our lives
that we may minister to the world in the name of Jesus,
through whom we pray. **Amen.**

INVITATION TO THE OFFERING

Isaiah declares, *Isa. 58:10*
If you offer your food to the hungry
    and satisfy the needs of the afflicted,
then your light shall rise in the darkness
    and your gloom be like the noonday.
Let us offer ourselves and our gifts to God.

PRAYER OF THANKSGIVING/DEDICATION

O God, *Matt. 6:4; 2 Cor. 5:21*
receive these gifts we offer
as a sign of the dedication of our lives.
We bring nothing of our own,
for all that we have is yours.
We give, not for the sake of earthly reward,
but for the secret reward only you may grant:
the joy of your righteousness;
through Jesus Christ, our Lord. **Amen.**

CHARGE

Go in peace, *2 Cor. 5:20b*
reconciled to God and to one another.

BLESSING

The God of reconciliation bless you,
the grace of our Lord Jesus Christ keep you,
and the power of the Holy Spirit strengthen you
this day and forevermore. *2 Cor. 5:20a*

Questions for Reflection

How can I give alms, pray, or fast without regard for the attention of others? How does Jesus' admonition to do these acts in secret compare to his earlier command in the Sermon on the Mount: "Let your light shine before others, so that they may see your good works and give glory to your Father in heaven" (Matt. 5:16)? What is the reward that God gives to those who give alms, pray, and fast?

Household Prayer: Morning

Dear God, you call me to repentance as I begin this new day.
If through careless ways I ignore your grace, O Lord,
prick my heart, shake me,
make me aware of your abiding presence,
and lead me in the way of everlasting life. Amen.

Household Prayer: Evening

[Pray Psalm 51:10]
Create in me a clean heart, O God,
And put a new and right spirit within me. Amen.

First Sunday in Lent

Deuteronomy 26:1–11   Romans 10:8b–13
Psalm 91:1–2, 9–16   Luke 4:1–13

OPENING WORDS / CALL TO WORSHIP

The God of our ancestors heard our cries   *Deut. 26:7, 8;*
and saw our oppression when we were slaves   *Ps. 91:1, 9, 15–16*
   in Egypt.
God brought us out with a mighty hand and
   an outstretched arm,
with signs and wonders God brought us through
   the wilderness.
The Lord, our shelter, our refuge, our dwelling place, says,
"When my people call to me, I will answer them;
I will be with them in trouble;
I will show them my salvation."
[or]
The season of Lent sets us on a journey.   *Luke 4:1; Rom. 10:8b*
The journey begins in the wilderness.
We follow the way of Jesus,
who faced trials, trouble, temptation, and testing.
Like Jesus, we are not alone.
The Holy Spirit is with us. God's Word is on our lips.
Our call is to trust in God alone,
to do God's will in all things.
For God leads us not only into the wilderness,
but also through the wilderness.*

---

*Jeffery L. Tribble, "Pastoral Perspective" on Luke 4:1–13, First Sunday in Lent, in ibid., 48.

CALL TO CONFESSION

God is faithful, leading us into freedom,
but we are conditioned to the slavery of sin.
Comfortable with the way things are,
we lose sight of the way God intends them to be.
We bring our confession before the One
who is more powerful than Pharaoh in Egypt,
mightier than the devil in the wilderness.

PRAYER OF CONFESSION

O God, our refuge and fortress,   *Ps. 91:2; Luke 4:4, 10;*
forgive us when we fail to trust in you.   *Rom. 10:10–11*
We fall to temptation;
we are swayed by false words;
we speak false words of our own.
We choose our ease and comfort
over your demanding claims upon us and upon the world.
In turning from you,
we settle for less than the abundant generosity you intend.
Forgive us, we pray.
Do not let us be put to shame, O God.
Hear us as we call to you and show us your salvation.
In Christ's name we pray. Amen.

DECLARATION OF FORGIVENESS

Scripture declares,   *Rom. 10:12, 13*
The Lord is generous to all who call on God's name.
Friends, believe the good news:
God does not turn away from us,
but desires to bring us into the glorious freedom
offered in Jesus Christ.
Everyone who calls on the name of the Lord will be saved.
Thanks be to God!

PRAYER OF THE DAY

God Most High,   *Ps. 91:1*
thank you for signs of your power and grace,
shown to us even in the wilderness.
Give us courage to stand firm in your Word
in every time of trial and testing,   *Luke 4:2, 12*

that we may enter the land of your freedom | *Deut. 26:9*
and receive the salvation you so generously give; | *Rom. 10:12–13*
through Jesus Christ our Lord. **Amen.**

PRAYER FOR ILLUMINATION

Bring your word near to us, O God.
May it rest not only on our lips, | *Rom. 10:8b*
but also reside in our hearts.
By the power of your Holy Spirit,
help us to respond to your word
with our whole lives
until you become our dwelling place; | *Ps. 91:9*
through Jesus Christ, we pray. **Amen.**

PRAYERS OF INTERCESSION

Almighty God,
we pray for all who live in places of threat and danger.
We trust in you,
for you are able to make peace in the midst of warfare
and turn rough places into level ground. | *Isa. 42:16*
Teach us to prepare a table where enemies may feast
    instead of fight. | *Ps. 23:5*
Hear our prayer, O God,
our refuge and fortress, our shelter and shade. | *Ps. 91:2*

We pray for those who do not have enough—
enough to eat, enough to wear, or enough justice.
We trust in you,
for you fill the empty with good things
and lift up the lowly. | *Luke 1:53, 5*
Help us to share the abundance we enjoy
and to work for the freedom and dignity of all your children.
Hear our prayer, O God,
our refuge and fortress, our shelter and shade.

We pray for all who are chronically homeless,
wandering our streets and sleeping unprotected;
and for those who are homeless for a season
because of natural disaster or economic trouble.

We trust in you,
for you give even to the sparrow a nest where she may lay
    her young. *Ps. 84:3*
Make us more determined to assist those who need
    a place to live.
Hear our prayer, O God,
our refuge and fortress, our shelter and shade.

We pray for those who suffer in body, mind, or heart.
We trust in you,
for you are able to heal
and to make whole in this life and the next.
Make us tender caregivers,
that your healing power may be at work in us and through us.
Hear our prayer, O God,
our refuge and fortress, our shelter and shade.

We pray for the church, dividing and uniting,
wavering and witnessing.
We trust in you,
for you called the church into being
and have made us your body in and for the world.
Keep your church from being both uncertain and too certain.
Help us to joyfully trust that the Spirit is leading us
into new opportunities of faith and service.
O God, our refuge and fortress, our shelter and shade,
we pray these things in the name of Jesus Christ,
who is generous to all who call upon him. Amen. *Rom. 10:12b*

INVITATION TO THE OFFERING

Israel came out of the wilderness
and into a land flowing with milk and honey.
There they were finally able to offer to God
baskets full, in joyful celebration.
We, too, bring the first fruits
of all that God has so generously given us,
with joy and thanksgiving.

PRAYER OF THANKSGIVING/DEDICATION

Gracious and Generous God,
we are amazed by the good gifts you bestow
     in abundance.
Thank you for food that sustains us on our journey.
Thank you for the company of saints to whom we
     are joined.
Thank you for giving us your work to do on earth.
We offer back to you a portion of all that we
     have received,
setting down our baskets in celebration of your
     greatest gift,
Jesus Christ, in whose name we pray. **Amen.**   *Deut. 26:4, 10*

CHARGE

These Lenten days will take us to the cross of Christ.
Go forward, knowing that you do not go this way alone.
Nor do we have to be afraid,
for the Word of God strengthens us and the Holy Spirit
     sustains us.

BLESSING

May the God of the Exodus lead us into freedom.
May the Holy Spirit bind us to God's will.
May Christ, God's only Son, show us the way of true
     justice and peace.

Question for Reflection

In Luke 4:1–13, the devil tempted Jesus to turn stones into bread, to take
control of the kingdoms of the world, and to perform a spectacular stunt
that would "wow the crowd." Jesus refused to take control in these ways.
Instead, Jesus chose another way to feed hungry people, to demonstrate
what the kingdom of God looks like, and to enter Jerusalem humbly. Why
do think Jesus chose another way to "do justice" and what are some ways
that you and your faith community practice justice in his name?

Household Prayer: Morning

Loving God, all night I slept in your shadow,   *Ps. 91:1; Deut. 28:8;*
    sheltered by you.   *Rom. 10:12*
As I enter into the gift of this day,
I trust that you are with me.
May I see signs and wonders of your presence in the
    world today,
for you alone are God.
I ask that this day afford me opportunities to celebrate
and share with others the abundance of your grace and love.
Help me to be open to all people you bring my way,
for you yourself make no distinctions,
but are Lord of all.
In Christ's name, I pray. Amen.

Household Prayer: Evening

God, my dwelling place, as the shadows fall, I rest in you.
Thank you for the faith that held me fast this day.
Thank you, too, for every person who offered me grace,
and for those to whom I could also show grace.
I pray this night for all who long to see a sign of your power
in the darkness that surrounds them.
Be near to them and show them your salvation.
And in the morning when I rise,
give me your work to do for another day;
in Jesus' name. Amen.

Second Sunday in Lent

Genesis 15:1–12, 17–18   Philippians 3:17–4:1
Psalm 27   Luke 13:31–35

OPENING WORDS / CALL TO WORSHIP

    The psalmist sings, *Ps. 27:4*
    One thing I asked of the LORD,
       that I will seek after:
    to live in the house of the LORD
       all the days of my life,
    to behold the beauty of the LORD,
       and to inquire in God's temple.
    Sisters and brothers, God is good,
    and in love and mercy greets us here.

CALL TO CONFESSION

    The Lord is our light and our salvation; *Ps. 27:1*
    whom shall we fear?
    With humble hearts,
    let us confess our sins before God and one another.

PRAYER OF CONFESSION

    Merciful God, *Phil. 3:20–21*
    you have made us citizens of heaven,
    but we confess that we have set our minds on
       earthly things.
    We have let our desire for security restrain our
       commitment to serve the poor.
    We have let our fear of danger curb our obligation
       to love our enemies.
    We have let our love of things dull our generosity
       to the needy.

We have let our craving for public status prevent our
    honesty about hidden sins.
Yet, you know the desires of our heart
and nothing is hidden from you.
By the power of the Holy Spirit,
conform our sin-weakened bodies to the glory of Christ,
that we may be the body of Christ for the world. Amen.

DECLARATION OF FORGIVENESS

God, our light and our salvation,   *Ps. 27:1*
does not forsake us or leave us with our sin.
In Christ we are forgiven
and offered the gift of healing repentance.
Thanks be to God!

PRAYER OF THE DAY

Loving God,   *Ps. 27:1, 5, 11, 14*
you save all who seek refuge in you.
Grant that we who know your salvation
may walk always in your light,
take courage in your faithfulness,
and rejoice in your astounding goodness to us.
Through Christ, by the power of the Holy Spirit, we pray. **Amen.**

PRAYER FOR ILLUMINATION

Lord,   Gen. 15:4–6
open your Word by your Holy Spirit,
so that we, like Abraham,
may believe your promises to us. **Amen.**

PRAYERS OF INTERCESSION.

In peace let us pray to the Lord saying,
    Lord have mercy.

For the church throughout the world,
that all who bear the name of Christ
may find true repentance for their sins
and walk in the ways of peace,
let us pray to the Lord.
Lord, have mercy.

For the nations of the world,
wherever there is poverty, war, or oppression of human spirit,
that all people may repent of the evil they do to one another,
let us pray to the Lord.
Lord, have mercy.

For the planet Earth, God's gift to humankind,
that we repent of selfish or thoughtless exploitation
and tend it with care so that all may share justly in its bounty,
let us pray to the Lord.
Lord, have mercy.

For the leaders of the nations,
that they may work for the common good of all people
and repent of arrogant nationalism,
let us pray to the Lord.
Lord, have mercy.

For our enemies,
that we may learn to love them with regard for God's compassion,
forgiving wrongs and seeking reconciliation,
let us pray to the Lord.
Lord, have mercy.

For those who are sick or in trouble,
for the defenseless, the weak, and the poor,
that they may find help in their time of need,
and that the church may heed their cry,
let us pray to the Lord.
Lord, have mercy.

Loving God,
hear the prayers of your people for the sake of our world.
With our prayers, accept the dedication of our lives
that we may minister to the world in the name of Jesus,
through whom we pray. **Amen.**

INVITATION TO THE OFFERING
Christ has given his life for us.
Let us offer ourselves and our gifts to God.

PRAYER OF THANKSGIVING/DEDICATION

O God, *Ps. 27:13*
we have beheld your goodness to us.
Accept the offering of the work of our hands,
and use us for the sake of Christ,
in whose name we pray. **Amen.**

CHARGE

Sisters and brothers,
stand firm in the Lord. *Phil. 4:1*

BLESSING

The God of reconciliation bless you,
the grace of our Lord Jesus Christ keep you,
and the power of the Holy Spirit strengthen you
this day and forevermore.

Questions for Reflection

In Luke 13:35 Jesus says, "And I tell you, you will not see me until
the time comes when you say, 'Blessed is the one who comes in the name
of the Lord.'" To what sort of "seeing" does Jesus refer? Is Jesus calling for
more than a verbal declaration that he is the Messiah? How might I live
so that I become a testimony that Jesus is truly the one who comes in the
name of God?

Household Prayer: Morning

Dear God,
I do not know all of the challenges that face me this day,
but still I pray:
if I should be tempted by desire for earthly gain,
remind me of my citizenship in heaven. *Phil. 4:1*
If I should be distracted by hunger,
satisfy me with your Holy Spirit until I hunger no more.
Let me walk in the way of Christ
so that my life testifies in deed and word,
"Blessed is the one who comes in the name of the Lord." Amen.

Household Prayer: Evening

Dear God,
great is your mercy to me,
even when I have not remembered you.
Where I have strayed from your path,
forgive my sins and show me the way to salvation.
Grant me rest this night
that I may rise refreshed in my commitment
to the way of my Lord, Jesus Christ,
in whose name I pray. Amen.

Third Sunday in Lent

Isaiah 55:1–9   1 Corinthians 10:1–13
Psalm 63:1–8   Luke 13:1–9

OPENING WORDS / CALL TO WORSHIP

Everyone who thirsts: *Isa. 55:1, 3, 6, 7*
Come to the waters,
seek the Lord,
repent and return
so that you may live.

All who are hungry for righteousness: *Isa. 55:7; Matt. 5:6*
Come to the waters,
seek the Lord,
repent and return
so that you may live.

All who need the help of God: *Ps. 63:7*
Come to the waters,
seek the Lord,
repent and return
so that you may live.

CALL TO CONFESSION

The Scriptures call us to turn from sinful ways   *Isa. 55:6–7*
and return to God,
who offers mercy and pardon.
Trusting in that mercy, let us call upon God who is near.

PRAYER OF CONFESSION

Holy God,   *Isa. 55:1–2, 8;*
we confess that we have grown complacent   *Luke 13:8*
in our response to you.

You set before us a rich feast of blessing,
but we are drawn to lesser things that cannot satisfy.
You call us to attend to urgent needs in the world,
but we indulge our own desires.
Our ways are not your ways;
our thoughts do not ascend to your thoughts.
Forgive us when we fall short of your claim upon our lives.
Disturb our complacency and quicken our desire
for a more fruitful life.
Be patient, we pray, as we amend who we are,
in the hope of becoming who you intend us to be.
We ask this in the name of our Savior,
your Son, Jesus Christ. Amen.

DECLARATION OF FORGIVENESS

God's love is sure and steadfast,   *Isa. 55:3; 1 Cor. 10:3, 13*
always providing a way out,
a way through,
a way back to God.
**Through the waters of baptism,
we have died with Christ and are raised with him.
With gratitude, in faith,
we will walk the way of Christ.**

PRAYER OF THE DAY

Your glory and power, O God,   *Ps. 63:1–7; John 4:10, 14*
surround us in the sanctuary.
We lift up our hands and call on your name.
We are your people,
thirsty for the living water you alone can give.
When we consider how you have helped us,
giving us a spring that gushes up to eternal life,
we cling to you,
singing praises with joyful lips;
through Jesus Christ, our Lord. **Amen.**

PRAYER FOR ILLUMINATION

We seek you in your word, O God,   *Ps. 63:1–5*
as though we are searching for water in a dry and
    weary land.

By the power of your Holy Spirit,
may this word be to us a rich feast,
satisfying the soul.
Then with our mouths, we will praise you;
and with our lives, we will bless you,
our Host and our Hope. **Amen.**

PRAYERS OF INTERCESSION

God of generous provision, *Isa. 55:2–3; Ps. 63:1, 5;*
we are grateful for the many ways you care for us *Luke 13:8*
and provide for the needs of your people.
In word, water, bread, and wine, you nourish and sustain us.
When we listen to you, we encounter delight,
and when we come to you, we live most fully.

Sometimes, though, we find ourselves in a dry and weary land . . .
    Where we have misused and depleted creation,
        drought and famine leave people and animals facing hunger
            and starvation.
    Where we have polluted streams, rivers, and oceans,
    fish and other water creatures suffer and die.
    People without access to clean water become sick.
    O God, help us to care for your creation in ways that
        make it possible
    for all to have enough food and water—life, verdant and abundant.

Sometimes we find ourselves in a dry and weary land . . .
    In places torn apart by war, where the earth itself has been ravaged;
    where hospitals and homes and corner stores have been reduced
        to rubble;
    where human lives have been destroyed and deformed;
    where peace lies in the ruins and hope is buried.
    O God, raise peace among us again.
    Build hope up from the ground.
    Restore in us and in the world's leaders
    the will and determination to make an end of war and a new
        beginning for justice.

Sometimes we find ourselves in a dry and weary land . . .
    When we are lost, unable to find our way to a place that is
        home for us;

when we are sad and weighed down with regret or grief;
when we are tired or sick in body, mind, or spirit.
O God, provide water in the desert and manna in the wilderness—
enough to sustain us for one more day,
even enough to revive us for the long haul.

Sometimes we find ourselves in the rich feast of your presence . . .
We celebrate a new beginning in our lives:
a new job, a new relationship, a new life,
a new day of sobriety, a second chance.
O God, we give thanks to you for this new blessing in our lives.

Sometimes we find ourselves in the rich feast of your presence . . .
We give thanks for the gift of healing after injury or illness;
for laughter that bubbles up to replace our tears;
for hope that spills its soothing light over the darkness of our
    despair.
O God, we thank you for the gift of wholeness and resurrection
promised to us in Jesus Christ.

Sometimes we find ourselves in the rich feast of your presence . . .
We enjoy the relief of forgiveness given and received;
we enjoy a breach in walls of division;
our own hearts are enlarged and our own vision is broadened by
    new understanding;
we welcome a prodigal home or are ourselves welcomed home again.
O God, we thank you that you are reconciling all things in heaven
and on earth.

Be patient with us, we pray, in the varied landscapes of our lives.
Make us patient with one another and even with ourselves.
Do your good work within us, among us, and beyond us, too,
until our lives and all of creation come fully into your realm.
You, who so generously provide, deserve our praise, our grateful praise.
In Jesus' name we pray. **Amen.**

INVITATION TO OFFERING
Disciples of Jesus, children of God,   *Isa. 55:2*
we often spend our money on that which is not true bread,
and labor toward things that will never satisfy.

In our offering, we give to things that are of God:
bread for the hungry,
good news for those who are oppressed,
the ministries of the church that welcome strangers and sons and
    daughters alike.
We bring before God a portion of all that God has so freely given to us.

PRAYER OF THANKSGIVING/DEDICATION

God of wilderness and Promised Land,
in days of want and in days of plenty
you have been with us.
By these gifts we now share,
may others know of your providence and care.
Send us—not only our offerings, but our very selves—
to console and comfort,
to lift up and reach out,
to listen and sit beside
your children everywhere
at the one Table you have set;
through Jesus Christ our Lord. **Amen.**

CHARGE

On this third Sunday of Lent, *Luke 13:7–8; Ps. 63:1*
we are urged to shake off the complacency that
    can overtake us;
to seek God as people in a dry and weary land seek water;
and to bear fruit in our daily lives
that contributes to God's kingdom of justice and love.

BLESSING

May the mercy of God ground us,
the love of Christ take root in us,
and the Holy Spirit grow in us,
that we may be ready for the coming of the kingdom.

Questions for Reflection

Luke 13:1–9 tells the story of a fruitless fig tree that the owner is ready to cut down. The gardener, however, asks for a little more time. The gardener wants to tend and cultivate the soil in the hope that figs may yet grow. The gardener is open to a different future for this tree, in spite of its present condition. Think about my own life, or the life of someone I love, in relationship to this story: What needs special tending? What will cultivate the "soil" of daily life so that new growth, new possibilities, might emerge? And what can I learn from this gardener about allowing for a different outcome, a new possibility?

Household Prayer: Morning

Gracious God,
this new day carries the potential for growth and new life.
Help me to attend to those things in me
that need care and attention.
Sow your word in me
that I may grow in faithfulness and understanding.
Shake me out of dull routines,
so that I may take part in the good news
you continue to tell urgently and passionately.
In Christ's name. Amen.

Household Prayer: Evening

As I lie down this night in the shadow of your wings,   *Ps. 63:7, 1, 5, 2, 3*
God of my life,
I know that you will be with me
even as you have helped me through this day.
Whether I am weary from the day,
or whether the day has been a rich feast of blessings,
I give thanks for your power and glory,
which are present in every circumstance.
As I give myself over to rest and sleep,
I remember that your steadfast love is better than life.
So, I pray, surround me with your love tonight and always.
In the peace of Christ I pray. Amen.

Fourth Sunday in Lent

Joshua 5:9–12   2 Corinthians 5:16–21
Psalm 32   Luke 15:1–3, 11b–32

OPENING WORDS / CALL TO WORSHIP
Grace and peace in Jesus Christ our Lord.
Amen.
Blessed are those whose transgression is forgiven.   *Ps. 32:1*
Thanks be to God.

CALL TO CONFESSION
Trusting the grace promised to us in Jesus Christ,
let us confess our sins before God and one another.

PRAYER OF CONFESSION
Merciful God,
we confess that we have strayed from your ways.   *Luke 15:11b–24*
Like the Prodigal Son, we have wasted our
**   inheritance.**
You gave us the earth for our home,
but we squander earth's resources and hoard
**   its bounty.**
You gave us neighbors to love, but we pursue selfish
**   ambitions.**
You gave us the commandments that lead to
**   human flourishing,**
but we break your law and forsake your love.
Forgive us our sin and bring us to repentance.
Draw our wandering hearts back to you
that we may find freedom in obedience to your love.
Through Christ our Lord we pray. Amen.

DECLARATION OF FORGIVENESS

As a parent welcomes home a wayward child, *Luke 15:20*
so God embraces all who return in true repentance.
In the name of Jesus Christ, we are forgiven.

PRAYER OF THE DAY

Gracious God, seeker of the lost: *Luke 15:20;*
draw your children back to your loving embrace, *2 Cor. 5:18–20*
restore us to our inheritance as daughters and sons,
and reconcile our hearts to you,
that we may become ambassadors
of your reconciling love to all the world.
Through Christ by the power of the Holy Spirit we pray. **Amen.**

PRAYER FOR ILLUMINATION

Almighty God, by your Holy Spirit *2 Cor. 5:16–17*
open our minds and bodies to the re-creating power
    of your Word,
that we may see the world though the mind of Christ
and live in the world as a foretaste of your new creation.
In Jesus' name we pray. **Amen.**

PRAYERS OF INTERCESSION

In peace let us pray to the Lord saying,
    Lord have mercy. *2 Cor. 5:18; Luke 15:20*

For the church throughout the world,
that all Christians may embody the reconciling
    love of Christ,
let us pray to the Lord.
Lord, have mercy.

For the nations of the world and its leaders,
that all may dwell in peace
and that justice may be tempered by mercy,
let us pray to the Lord.
Lord, have mercy.

For the planet Earth, God's gift to humankind,
that all may share wisely its resources

and conserve its riches for our children's children,
let us pray to the Lord.
Lord, have mercy.

For our enemies,
that we may regard them with the reconciling love
made manifest in Christ,
let us pray to the Lord.
Lord, have mercy.

For those who are sick or in trouble,
for the defenseless, the weak, and the poor,
that they may be restored to wholeness of life and livelihood,
let us pray to the Lord.
Lord, have mercy.

For the lost,
for those who have abandoned God, friends, or family,
and for those who have never known such love,
that they may come to know the joy of love's embrace,
let us pray to the Lord.
Lord, have mercy.

Loving God, hear the prayers of your people
for the sake of our world,
and our Savior Jesus Christ, through whom we pray.
Amen.

INVITATION TO THE OFFERING
As people of the New Creation,
let us offer ourselves and our gifts to God.

PRAYER OF THANKSGIVING/DEDICATION
O God, all that we have comes from you.
Receive this offering and with it the offering of our lives,
for we return to you only what you have so graciously given.
Use us for the sake of Christ,
in whose name we pray. **Amen.**

CHARGE

> Go forth as ambassadors for Christ,   *2 Cor. 5:20*
> in whom we have new life.

BLESSING

> The God of reconciliation bless you,   *2 Cor. 5:19*
> the grace of our Lord Jesus Christ keep you,
> and the power of the Holy Spirit strengthen you this day and
>   forevermore.

Questions for Reflection

In what ways am I like the Prodigal Son? In what ways am I like the elder son?

Household Prayer: Morning

Loving God, in all I do this day,   *2 Cor. 5:16*
use me as a sign of your reconciling love.
Let me not view anyone from a human point of view,
but let me see all whom I will encounter with the eyes of Christ,
through whom I pray. Amen.

Household Prayer: Evening

Merciful God, if like the Prodigal Son   *Luke 15:11b–24*
I have strayed from you this day,
call me back to your loving embrace.
If like the elder son,
I have harbored resentment for the grace you give to others,
reprove me.
Help me claim in thought and deed the inheritance of the saints
who share with Jesus compassion and forgiveness to all who lose
    their way. Amen.

Fifth Sunday in Lent

Isaiah 43:16–21   Philippians 3:4b–14
Psalm 126   John 12:1–8

OPENING WORDS / CALL TO WORSHIP
As people formed by God, we give praise to God:
Dry ground in the sea,
rivers in the desert,
Christ among us—
God is doing a new thing!

As people restored by God, we give praise to God:
Dry ground in the sea,
rivers in the desert,
Christ among us—
God is doing a new thing!

As people pressing on in faith, we give praise to God:
Dry ground in the sea,
rivers in the desert,
Christ among us—
God is doing a new thing!
[or]
When the Lord restored the fortunes of Zion,   *Ps. 126*
we were like those who dream.
Then our mouth was filled with laughter and shouts of joy.
We rejoiced: "The Lord has done great things for us."
May those who go out weeping, bearing the seed for sowing,
come home with joy, carrying their sheaves.

CALL TO CONFESSION

If we ask God to restore us to the way we have been,
then we have not asked for as much as God intends to give.
God is not content simply to return or restore us to former
   things.
Instead, God seeks to give the gift of resurrection—a new and
   abundant life.
With confidence in God's generosity,
we confess our sins and seek the new life offered in Jesus Christ.*

PRAYER OF CONFESSION

Purifying God,
we grow comfortable with the way things are
in our lives, in the church, and in the world.
We do not always welcome the new life you offer in Christ,
for you overturn our notions of power and protocol.
Sure of our own righteousness, we are critical of others.
Wanting to control our assets,
we hoard the gifts you give us.
Forgive us, we pray, for seeking our gain at the expense of others.
Help us bend our lives toward your own life of self-giving and
   sacrifice.
Fill us, our homes and churches, the whole world,
with the abundant love of Christ until all are made new.
In Christ's name, we pray. Amen.

DECLARATION OF FORGIVENESS

The apostle Paul reminds us that we do not make ourselves
   righteous.   *Phil. 3:9*
Our righteousness comes through faith in Christ,
who has made us his own.
Hear the good news!
In Jesus Christ we are forgiven.
The old life has passed away—and a new life has begun.

Forgetting what lies behind,   *Phil. 3:13–14*
and straining forward to what lies ahead,
we press on toward the heavenly call of God in Christ Jesus.

*Kimberly L. Clayton, "Pastoral Perspective" on Psalm 126, Fifth Sunday in Lent,
in ibid., 132.

PRAYER OF THE DAY

Creator God,   *Isa. 43:21b; Ps. 126:2–6*
you have formed us as your own,
so whether we are weeping or laughing,
dreaming or shouting for joy,
we are always coming home to you.
For all this and more, we thank you in Jesus' name. **Amen.**

PRAYER FOR ILLUMINATION

Break open the Scripture through the power of your Spirit,
   O God.   *John 12:3*
Let your word, read and proclaimed,
pour out until its fragrance fills this house and our lives.
Then, anointed with your word,
send us out to share the good news we have received.
We pray in the name of Jesus Christ, who is with us always. **Amen.**

PRAYERS OF INTERCESSION

God our Provider,   *Isa. 43:16, 19; Ps. 126:2,*
out of your fullness you cause life to spring up   *5–6; Rev. 21:5*
   in barren landscapes;
you have power to control troubled waters, making
   a path of safety;
you hear our cries and receive our tears;
you restore us to joy and laughter.
You have done great things for us, O God,
and are continually making all things new.
We thank you, O God:
You are making all things new.

We thank you for the gift of your Son, Jesus Christ,
whose life and ministry has guided us through this Lenten season
and guides us in every season of life.
In his suffering and death,
he knows full well the troubles and pains we face in this earthly life.
In his resurrection is the hope of our own.
Surrounded by your overflowing love, we are not alone.
We thank you, O God:
You are making all things new.

With thanksgiving we celebrate your care
and the gift of newness in our lives:
for recovery from illness or injury;
for calm after a time of unrest or turmoil;
for a sense of direction after uncertainty;
for new life;
for new opportunities.
We thank you, O God:
You are making all things new.

We pray for people who wait in difficult places.
For those who are suffering and those at life's end;
for people struggling with employment and financial worries;
for those estranged from loved ones;
for those trapped in the grip of addiction;
for people enduring emotional or spiritual turmoil.
Because you are able to make a way in every wilderness,
we thank you, O God:
You are making all things new.

We pray for the needs of the world.
May peace invade places of war
and justice crowd out oppression and cruelty.
Protect soldiers and citizens alike from harm's way
and make all conflict cease.
Bless leaders of communities, states, and nations,
that they may speak the truth and work with others for
    the common good.
Pour out healing on the earth itself,
depleted and injured by our careless consumption and
    intentional greed.
Comfort those devastated by natural disasters;
strengthen those supplying shelter, food, and aid.
Amid the chaos of this world, your Spirit intercedes
with sighs too deep for words.
We thank you, O God:
You are making all things new.

We pray for the church, the body of Christ in the world,
that we may proclaim your Word boldly.

Lead us, by the power of your Spirit, to witness to your truth,
for we remember and proclaim that death does not have the last word—
in our lives, in the church, or in the world.
We thank you, O God:
You are making all things new!

We pray in the name of Jesus Christ, crucified and risen. Amen.

INVITATION TO OFFERING

As it is written in Deuteronomy:
"Since there will never cease to be some in need on the earth,
I therefore command you,
'Open your hand to the poor and needy neighbor . . . .'"
Through our tithes and offerings,
we can give generously, as Mary did,
and remember the poor.
As we open wide our hands, we attend to Christ himself,
who is present especially among those considered the least and the lost.
Let us offer to God these gifts for ministry in Christ's name.

PRAYER OF THANKSGIVING/DEDICATION

Abundant God: You cause water to flow in   *Isa. 43:19; John 2:1–11;*
   desert places.   *6:1–14; 12:3*
You give wine to flow at a wedding feast,
and food to feed five thousand on a grassy mountainside.
Your generosity astounds and humbles us.
We bow before you in gratitude and awe,
asking you to receive what we have brought in response.
May these gifts be a pleasing and fragrant offering,
for the sake of the world you came to save.
We pray in your holy name. **Amen.**

CHARGE

By her gift, Mary prepared for the day of Jesus' burial.
By our prayers and presence,
we prepare for this Lenten turn toward Palm Sunday and Holy Week.
Remembering that our fickle passions and mixed motives
are no match for the steadfast love of God, we continue the journey
   to the cross.
[or]

As the season of Lent turns toward Palm Sunday and the events
   of Holy Week,
go forth remembering both Mary's faithfulness and Judas's betrayal
as you consider your own life of discipleship.*

BLESSING

May God guide you through the desert places,   *Isa. 43:19b;*
may Christ lead you into knowing him more deeply,   *Phil. 3:10*
and the Holy Spirit fill you with faith overflowing:
that as you share in Christ's suffering,
you will also trust the power of his resurrection.

Questions for Reflection

John 12:1–8 draws our attention to three people: Mary, Judas, and Jesus.
It is easy enough to identify Mary as "the good disciple" and Judas as "the
bad disciple" not only in this story but also in the larger story of Jesus' life
and death. We can (and do) make this judgment: Mary is accepted and
affirmed, while Judas is rejected. But is this the judgment that the other
person in the story would make? As one commentator puts it, ". . . if Jesus
came to save the lost, surely there is no one in the gospel story who is more
lost than the one who betrays Jesus. . . . If the Good Shepherd can and does
go to any length to save a lost sheep, is Judas beyond the saving grasp of the
Good Shepherd?"[†] This is not a question with an easy answer. As this story
ushers you into Holy Week, consider how the cross, the grace of Christ,
speaks to this story and to your own life story, which like most life stories
may not be a simple "either/or" example of faithfulness, but a "both/and"
mix of faithfulness and unfaithfulness.

Household Prayer: Morning

Merciful God, as I begin this day,
place in me a spirit of generosity
so that I may freely share love, joy, and encouragement
with those I encounter.

---

*George Stoup, "Theological Perspective" on John 12:1–8, Fifth Sunday in Lent, in
  ibid., 144.
[†]Ibid., 142, 144.

Keep me from quick judgments
so that I leave room for your grace in my life and in the lives of others.
Make me your faithful disciple in my words and in my actions,
as well as in the thoughts of my heart; in Jesus' name. Amen.

Household Prayer: Evening

All through the day, Lord Jesus, you have been present.
As I settle into the routines of home and evening,
I long to be at home in my relationship with you.
Help me to put aside the cares of the day and the worries of tomorrow
in order to fully enjoy the peace of your presence now.
I pray that your peace will also be with those I know
who have special need of your care tonight,
and I pray for those who lie down this night without the safety
    of home or bed,
without enough food or resources.
Bring your light into the surrounding darkness
so that all of us may sleep in the security of your love. Amen.

Palm Sunday / Passion Sunday

LITURGY OF THE PALMS

Psalm 118:1–2, 19–29   Luke 19:28–40

LITURGY OF THE PASSION

Isaiah 50:4–9a   Philippians 2:5–11
Psalm 31:9–16   Luke 22:14–23:56 *or* 23:1–49

OPENING WORDS / CALL TO WORSHIP

They brought the colt of a donkey to Jesus;   *Luke 19:35–40*
and after throwing their cloaks on the colt,
they set Jesus on it.
**As he rode along, people kept spreading their cloaks
    on the road.**
As he was now approaching the path down from the
    Mount of Olives,
the whole multitude of the disciples began to praise God
joyfully with a loud voice
for all the deeds of power that they had seen, saying,
**"Blessed is the king who comes in the name of the Lord!
Peace in heaven, and glory in the highest heaven!"**
Some of the Pharisees in the crowd said to him,
"Teacher, order your disciples to stop."
He answered them:
"I tell you, if these were silent, the stones would shout out."

CALL TO CONFESSION

Let us confess our sin to our God,   *Ps. 118:2*
trusting that God's steadfast love endures forever.

PRAYER OF CONFESSION

God of heaven and earth,
we give you thanks for sending us Jesus Christ
    in your name.   *Luke 19:38*
Even though we profess to follow him,
we confess that in times of trial we too often deny him.   *Luke 22:61*

**Forgive us and heal us, we pray.
Help us to put our faith not in the princes of this world,
but only in the Prince of Peace.** *Ps. 118:9*
In Jesus' name we pray. Amen.

DECLARATION OF FORGIVENESS

It is the Lord who helps us; who will declare us guilty? *Isa. 50:9a*
Because of the grace we received in baptism,
we have nothing to fear.
Forgiven and freed,
let us share the peace of Christ with one another.

PRAYER OF THE DAY

Gracious God, as we enter this Holy Week,
strengthen us to move beyond
the festive parade of palms
and to follow Jesus into the way of the cross,
that united with him and all the faithful,
we may one day enter through the gates of righteousness *Ps. 118:19*
into the eternal city, the New Jerusalem, *Rev. 21:2*
where we may praise you with Christ and the
 Holy Spirit forever. **Amen.**

PRAYER FOR ILLUMINATION

Eternal God,
quiet within us all mortal voices, *Ps.118:8*
that through the story of the passion and
by the power of your Holy Spirit,
we may have the same mind that was in Christ Jesus, *Phil. 2:5*
in whose name we pray. **Amen.**

PRAYERS OF INTERCESSION

God in the highest,
you came to us in a human being
who humbled himself like a slave. *Phil. 2:7–8*
**The stone that the builders rejected
has become the chief cornerstone.** *Ps. 118:22*
We pray for the nations that worship power and might;
may they be ruled by humility and peace.

**The stone that the builders rejected
has become the chief cornerstone.**
We pray for the church and its leaders,
that we may have the mind of Christ.   *Phil. 2:5*
**The stone that the builders rejected
has become the chief cornerstone.**
We pray for the victims of human tragedies and
    disasters of nature.
**The stone that the builders rejected
has become the chief cornerstone.**
We pray for those who are in prison—
the repentant and the unrepentant
and those falsely accused.   *Luke 23:32*
**The stone that the builders rejected
has become the chief cornerstone.**
We pray for those who are ill or infirmed
or are rejected because they are seen to be weak.
**The stone that the builders rejected
has become the chief cornerstone.**
God of compassion,
through Jesus Christ you have come to us and shared
    our common lot.
Mold us into people who show your mercy
and keep us obedient to him whose name is above
    all other names—   *Phil. 2:9*
Jesus Christ, in whose name we pray. **Amen.**

INVITATION TO THE OFFERING
God has given us his only Child, Jesus Christ,
as the way of our salvation.
Let us then give generously, as God has given to us.

PRAYER OF THANKSGIVING/DEDICATION
Holy One,
we give you thanks for the great deeds of salvation
that you have done and continue to do.
Bless these offerings of thanksgiving
that they may further your kingdom in this world;
through Jesus Christ we pray. **Amen.**

CHARGE

Let the same mind be in you that was in Christ Jesus.   *Phil. 2:5*

[or]

Go in peace,
trusting in Christ's promise that
we will be with him in paradise.   *Luke 23:42*

BLESSING

May you know the love of Christ,
the mercy of the Father,
and the fire of the Spirit
as you go with the One God
who is Mother of us all.

Questions for Reflection

The events of Holy Week make up the central story of our faith. Can we see the suffering of others in our world in the passion of Jesus? What are some ways that the daughters and sons of humanity are crucified today? How are we called to respond?

Household Prayer: Morning

God, as I enter into this new day,
I ask that you keep me mindful
of the profound nature of this Holy Week.
Help me to go beyond the joyful parade of the palms
and to follow Jesus into the suffering of this world,
mindful that he was obedient to you, even to the cross. Amen.

Household Prayer: Evening

Thank you, God, for the gift of this day.
If I remembered today my betrayals of you,
remind me now of your steadfast love for me,
as I give this day into your hands and rest in peace. Amen.

Holy Thursday

Exodus 12:1–4 (5–10), 11–14   1 Corinthians 11:23–26
Psalm 116:1–2, 12-19   John 13:1–17, 31b–35

OPENING WORDS / CALL TO WORSHIP
Jesus said,
"I give you a new commandment, that you love one another.
Just as I have loved you,
you also should love one another.
By this everyone will know that you are my disciples,
if you have love for one another."   *John 13:34–35*

CALL TO CONFESSION
In all humility
and faith in the grace of God,
let us confess our sin.

PRAYER OF CONFESSION
[Allow a lengthy silence between biddings.]

Holy and gracious God,
our sin is too heavy to bear.
Trusting in your mercy,
we lay before you the truth of who we are.

We confess our failure to love as Christ loved . . .

We confess our covetousness and greed . . .

We confess our weakness before temptation . . .

We confess our frailty before the challenges of this world . . .

134

Merciful God, forgive us.
Heal us, and make us whole,
for the sake of your Son, our Savior,
Jesus Christ, in whose name we pray. **Amen.**

DECLARATION OF FORGIVENESS

The saying is sure and worthy of full acceptance,
that Christ Jesus came into the world to
save sinners. *1 Tim. 1:15*
Sisters and brothers, believe the gospel:
in Jesus Christ, we are forgiven.

PRAYER OF THE DAY

Holy One, now is the time in which Jesus is glorified,
and you are glorified in him. *John 13:31*
Empower us to love as Jesus loved,
so that everyone will know
that we follow the way of Jesus Christ, our friend
and savior. **Amen.** *John 13:34–35*

PRAYER FOR ILLUMINATION

God of Exodus and Resurrection, *Jer. 31:33–34*
you have promised to write your law on our hearts.
As we hear the reading of your Word,
teach us your law of love,
that by the power of your Holy Spirit,
we may show forth the light of Christ,
in whose name we pray. **Amen.**

FOOTWASHING

*[Worshipers may wash one another's feet, pouring water over them
and drying them with a towel. This may be done in silence or
accompanied by singing.]*

PRAYERS OF INTERCESSION

O God most high, on this night we
remember Jesus *John 13:15, 17, 35*
humbly washing the feet of his disciples.
**Jesus has set an example for us; help us to
follow him.**

We pray for the church and for all who serve others,
especially those in most need.
Jesus has set an example for us; help us to follow him.
We pray for peace among nations and religions,
and peace among people.
Jesus has set an example for us; help us to follow him.
We pray for those who suffer
because of hatred and hard-heartedness.
Jesus has set an example for us; help us to follow him.
We pray for those who are injured
by acts of violence or natural disaster.
Jesus has set an example for us; help us to follow him.
We pray for those who are sick or dying,
for those who are frightened or distraught.
Jesus has set an example for us; help us to follow him.
Most holy God,
in Jesus Christ you show us that true glory is in humble service.
Renew in us your call to love one another,
to welcome the stranger,
and to show Christ's mercy in all we do.
It is for his sake that we pray. **Amen.**

INVITATION TO OFFERING

What shall I return to the Lord for all God's bounty
   to me?   *Ps. 116:12, 14*
**I will pay my vows to the Lord in the presence
   of all the people.**
With humble and grateful hearts, let us bring our
   offerings to God.

PRAYER OF THANKSGIVING/DEDICATION

Gracious God,
you pour out blessing upon us and cover us with grace.
Accept these offerings,
that they may bring blessing to those who need them,
and give witness to your overwhelming love;
in Jesus' name. **Amen.**

CHARGE

Go out into the world to love as Jesus loved.

BLESSING

May the grace of our Lord Jesus Christ,   *1 Cor. 13:13*
the love of God,
and the communion of the Holy Spirit
be with you this night and forevermore.

Question for Reflection

How has following Jesus redefined the meaning of "glory" and "majesty" in your life?

Household Prayer: Morning

God, this morning I pause to remember
all the times in my life when you have answered my prayers
and delivered me when I have stumbled.
Help me to see the opportunities before me today
to return your blessings to me
by being of service to others;
in Jesus' name. Amen.

Household Prayer: Evening

Thank you, God, for being with me today. For that I praise you!
I am your servant, God, for you have unloosed my bonds.
Forgive any times today when I forgot to walk in your ways.
Now as I turn to sleep, my soul is at rest,
for I trust in your mercy,
secure in the promise that I am precious to you. Amen.

Good Friday

Isaiah 52:13–53:12   Hebrews 10:16–25 *or*
                                  Hebrews 4:14–16; 5:7–9
Psalm 22   John 18:1–19:42

[These texts are offered to supplement, but not necessarily replace, the ancient and ecumenical liturgies of Good Friday, particularly the Solemn Intercession and the Solemn Reproaches of the Cross, which are found in the service books of various denominations.]

OPENING WORDS / CALL TO WORSHIP
On this Good Friday,
we contemplate the good news of the cross:
how Christ our Lord stretched out his arms
to embrace a world of suffering and sin;
how Christ our Lord stretched out his arms
to save us.

Come and see the beloved Son of God.   *Isa. 52:13*
He is high and lifted up.
Come and see the Ruler of the nations.
He is high and lifted up.
Come and see the Savior of the world.
He is high and lifted up—upon a cross.
[or]
Beside the gate, a woman asked Simon Peter   *John 18:16–17, 25, 27*
if he was a disciple of Jesus.
He said, "I am not."
Later they asked him again,
"You are not also one of his disciples, are you?"
Peter denied it and said, "I am not."
Then one of the slaves of the high priest asked,
"Did I not see you in the garden with him?"
Again, Peter denied it. *[Ring a bell three times.]*

CALL TO CONFESSION

Since we have a high priest *Heb. 4:15–16*
who can sympathize with our weaknesses,
but we have one who in every respect
has been tested as we are, yet without sin,
let us therefore approach the throne of grace with boldness,
so that we may receive mercy
and find grace to help in time of need.

[or, at the font]

Since we have a great high priest over the house
    of God— *Heb. 10:21–23*
Jesus Christ our Savior—
let us approach God with a true heart
in full assurance of faith,
with our hearts sprinkled clean
from an evil conscience
and our bodies washed with pure water.
Let us hold fast to the confession of our hope without wavering,
for God who has promised is faithful.

PRAYER OF CONFESSION

[Alternate: use the Solemn Reproaches of the Cross]
Christ Jesus was despised and rejected.
We thought nothing of him.
He was oppressed and afflicted.
We hid our faces from him.
He bore our sickness and sin.
We believed God was punishing him.
We, like sheep, have gone astray. *Isa. 53:6*
Yet he, like a lamb, was led to the slaughter.
[silent confession]
Lamb of God, have mercy on us.
Lamb of God, grant us peace. Amen.

DECLARATION OF FORGIVENESS

Surely, Jesus Christ has borne our sin. *Isa. 53:4-5*
By his wounds we are healed.

[or]

This is the new covenant I make with you, says
    the Lord: *Heb. 10:16–17*

I will put my law in your hearts;
I will remember your sin no more.
Friends, believe the good news of the gospel:
In Jesus Christ we are forgiven.
Thanks be to God.

PRAYER OF THE DAY

Lord God, on this haunting holy day   *John 18–19*
we come to the place of the skull,
the place of the cross,
the place of our salvation.
In the face of such suffering,
show us the face of our Savior.
In the shadow of such evil,
show us the light of your grace;
through Jesus Christ our Lord. **Amen.**

PRAYER FOR ILLUMINATION

Holy God,   *John 19:30, 35*
as we bow our heads beneath the cross
pour out your Holy Spirit upon us
to testify to the truth
so that we may believe;
this we pray through Jesus Christ,
your Word made flesh. **Amen.**

PRAYERS OF INTERCESSION

[Alternate: use the Solemn Intercessions]

[Possible response to each intercession:]
O Lord, do not be far away;   *Ps. 22:19*
come quickly to help!

In the days of his flesh,   *Heb. 5:7; 4:14*
Jesus offered up prayers and supplications,
with loud cries and tears,
to the One who was able to save him from death.
Now we have a great high priest
who has passed through the heavens,

Jesus, the Son of God,
in whose name we pray:

We pray for all who are despised and rejected,   *Isa. 53:3, 7*
suffering and wounded, oppressed and afflicted.

We pray for all who feel forsaken,   *Ps. 22:1–2*
crying out by day and night: Where is my God?

We pray for those who are mocked and scorned,   *Ps. 22:6–7;*
the subjects of insult and injury.   *John 19:15*

We pray for all who hunger and thirst,   *Ps. 22:15, 17;*
whose mouths are dry, whose bodies waste away.   *John 19:28*

We pray for all who face the end of life,   *Ps. 22:15; John 19:30*
who lie in the dust of death.

We pray all these things in the name of Jesus Christ our Lord,
source of all healing and endless life. **Amen.**

INVITATION TO THE OFFERING
Christ gave his own life for the life of the world.
As Christ's body,
we are called to give our lives for others,
stretching out our hands
to share the gifts we have received.

PRAYER OF THANKSGIVING/DEDICATION
We give you thanks and praise, O God,
for your saving love,
poured out for us in Jesus Christ.
Receive these gifts we offer—
use them to help those who are suffering
and to show the good news of salvation;
through Jesus Christ our Lord. **Amen.**

DISMISSAL

Jesus said, "It is finished."   *John 19:30*

[All depart in silence.]

Question for Reflection

According to John, Jesus' last words on the cross are, "It is finished." The last words of Psalm 22 are "[God] has done it." What is finished? What has God done? Why do we call this day "Good Friday"? Where is the good news in the story of the cross?

Household Prayer: Morning

Hold us fast, God our Savior,
as the curtain of night is torn,
and this dark day approaches.
Hold us fast, God our Savior,
as our faith and hope are tested
and we await the rising sun. Amen.

Household Prayer: Evening

Holy God,
enthroned on the praises of your people,
we cry to you by day
and call on you by night.
Do not be far from us,
for trouble is near
and there is no one else to help. Amen.

Easter Day

Acts 10:34–43
or Isaiah 65:17–25
Psalm 118:1–2, 14–24

1 Corinthians 15:19–26
or Acts 10:34–43
John 20:1–18 *or* Luke 24:1–12

GREETING
[From the doors of the church]
Early on the first day of the week,   *Luke 24:1; John 20:1*
the disciples of Jesus went to the tomb
where he had been buried
only to find that the stone had been rolled away
and the tomb was empty.
Friends, we gather here as Christ's disciples,
on the first day of the week,
to celebrate the good news of the gospel:
Jesus Christ has risen from the dead!

OPENING WORDS / CALL TO WORSHIP
Rejoice and be glad: *Ps. 118:24; Isa. 65:17–18*
This is the day that the Lord has made!
Rejoice and be glad:
Heaven and earth will never be the same!
Rejoice and be glad:
Christ is risen! Alleluia!
[or]
People of God, we are witnesses to these things:
that Christ died, hanging on a cross;
that God raised him from the dead on the third day;
that he is coming again in glory to reign.
This is the good news we tell to all the world:
Jesus Christ is risen indeed! Alleluia!

CALL TO CONFESSION

Since sin and death came through a human being, 1 Cor. 15:21–22
the resurrection of the dead has also come through
  a human being.
For as all die in Adam,
all will be made alive in Christ.

Trusting in that promise of God,
let us confess our sin.
[or]

We know that God shows no partiality, *Acts 10:34*
but welcomes and forgives all those who repent
  and believe.

Let us confess our sin.

PRAYER OF CONFESSION

Gracious God, we have heard the good news:
how on the third day, Christ rose again.
Still we look for the living among the dead.
You rolled away the stone from the tomb.
Still we look for the living among the dead.
You sent messengers to proclaim the gospel.
Still we look for the living among the dead.
You were faithful to your promise;
you have done wonderful things!
Still we look for the living among the dead.

[silent confession]

Forgive us, Lord, we pray.
Teach us to trust your promise
and to believe the good news of salvation:
Christ is alive; Jesus is risen from the dead. Amen.

DECLARATION OF FORGIVENESS

When Christ comes to reign, *1 Cor. 15:24–26*
he will put an end to every ruler, every power,
  every authority;

he will put every enemy under his feet.
And the last enemy to be destroyed is death.

As we await that great and glorious day,
we rejoice in the good news of the gospel:
In Jesus Christ we are forgiven!
Thanks be to God.
[or]
Hear what the prophets have spoken: *Acts 10:43*
that everyone who believes in Christ
receives forgiveness of sins through his name.

Friends, believe the good news:
In Jesus Christ we are forgiven. Alleluia!

PRAYER OF THE DAY
Alleluia! We praise you, O God,
for the power of your saving love
revealed in the resurrection of our Lord.
As you have raised Jesus from the dead
give to us the gift of everlasting life,
that we may worship you forever;
through Christ, our risen Savior. **Amen.**

PRAYER FOR ILLUMINATION
Living God, by your Holy Spirit,
open our eyes to see the new light of this day;
open our lips to tell of the empty tomb;
open our hearts to believe the good news;
through Jesus Christ our Lord. **Amen.**

PRAYERS OF INTERCESSION
[Possible response to each intercession:]
Living God, hear our prayer: *Isa. 65:18–25*
Make of this world your new creation!

Before we call, you answer, O Lord.
Before we speak, you know our words.

Let there be joy in Jerusalem,
and peace among all nations.

Let sounds of weeping and cries of distress
turn to shouts of joy and laughter.

Let infants grow and thrive;
let the old dance like children.

Let every person find a home
and enjoy the fruit of their labor.

Let the wolf and the lamb live in peace;
let no one hurt or destroy another.

Show us, O God, the holy mountain you have prepared,
the new heaven and new earth you have promised,
so that we may be glad and rejoice in your presence forever;
through Jesus Christ, our risen Lord. **Amen.**

INVITATION TO THE OFFERING
We belong to Christ Jesus;   *1 Cor. 15:23, 25*
all things are his, for he is Lord of all.

PRAYER OF THANKSGIVING/DEDICATION
We praise you, O God, and give you thanks
that you have given us such joy, such grace, and such hope,
in the resurrection of Jesus Christ our Lord.
Let our lives be proof of that good news.
Let all our words and actions, our love and service
bear witness to your resurrection power;
for the sake of our living Lord, Jesus Christ. **Amen.**

CHARGE
Go out with joy to tell good news:
Jesus Christ is risen!
Alleluia!
[or]

You are witnesses to the resurrection;
you are messengers of the gospel.
Go forth to tell the good news,
preaching peace by Jesus Christ—
he is Lord of all.

BLESSING

Grace and peace to all   *Eph. 6:23–24*
who have an undying love
for our living Lord, Jesus Christ.

Questions for Reflection

What difference does it make to believe that Jesus Christ is risen from the
dead? How does your faith in the resurrection of Jesus Christ change the
way you think about sin and death? How does it change the way you live?

Household Prayer: Morning

God of endless life,
in the light of this new day
we see the dawning of your new creation.
Give us wonder and delight
to enjoy this day that you have made;
through Jesus Christ, our living Lord. Amen.

Household Prayer: Evening

Stay with us, Lord, for it is evening
and the day is almost over.
Help us to know that you are with us—
through the promise of your Word,
in the sharing of a meal,
and by the power of your Spirit
that burns within our hearts.
Bless and keep us, this night and always. Amen.

Second Sunday of Easter

Acts 5:27–32	Revelation 1:4–8
Psalm 118:14–29 *or* Psalm 150	John 20:19–31

OPENING WORDS / CALL TO WORSHIP

Christ is risen! *Ps. 150*
Christ is risen indeed!
Alleluia! Celebrate God in this sacred space!
Celebrate God in all places under heaven!
Give praise for God's mighty deeds!
Give praise for God's resurrecting power!
Praise God with a fanfare of trumpets.
Praise God with the harp and the cello!
Praise God with tambourines and dancing!
Praise God with flutes and guitars!
Praise God with cymbals and drums!
Let everything with life and breath praise God!

CALL TO CONFESSION

When we keep our fears and faults locked up inside us, *John 20:19, 26*
it is hard to be healed and receive new life.
So let us open ourselves to God in confession,
trusting the Lord's desire to give us peace.

PRAYER OF CONFESSION

God of the empty tomb and our empty hearts, *John 20:19–27*
when we are afraid to speak our faith in the world,
forgive us and help us to find our voice.
When we are afraid to forgive and to love again,
forgive us and give us the power to forgive.
When we are afraid to stand up to misguided authority,
join with the weak to make us all strong.

When we are confined by our hurts,
touch us with your wounded hands and set us free.
When we are locked behind our doubts and fears,
pass through our barricades, open our hearts, and
give us peace. Amen.

DECLARATION OF FORGIVENESS

Christ comes with healing light   *John 20:21–22, 31*
into our locked places and shadowy hurts,
resurrecting our spirits and breathing into us new life.
As God's own forgiven people,
go to bring peace, forgiveness, and new life to the world
in the name of Jesus Christ.

PRAYER OF THE DAY

God of the Resurrection, you open the tomb   *Ps. 150; John 20:22,*
and invite us to sing and dance in the   *27, 31*
new life you give us.
In Jesus Christ,
whose wounds are not erased but glorified in resurrection,
touch our wounds that they may be transformed
into channels of healing for others.
Holy Spirit, breathe into us the power to forgive so that all
may have new life.
In the name of Jesus we pray. **Amen.**

PRAYER FOR ILLUMINATION

Living God,   *John 20:29*
as the risen Christ came into the locked room of
the first disciples,
may your Word enter into us,
by the power of your Holy Spirit,
so that we who have not seen may yet believe. **Amen.**

PRAYERS OF INTERCESSION

Holy One, you have made us and redeemed us
through Christ
to be your kingdom and your priests,
serving you and your dominion forever and ever.   *Rev. 1:5–6*

Help us to be wounded healers who bring your peace
    into the world.   *John 20:21*
As you sent Christ, now send us.

We pray for the church around the world in all its
    local expressions,
that we and our leaders may truly be your kingdom
    and your priests,   *Rev. 1:6*
serving not ourselves but your glory and your dominion.
As you sent Christ, now send us.

We pray for those who cannot see you and yet desire
    to believe.   *John 20:29*
As you sent Christ, now send us.

We pray for religious and secular authorities
who speak truth to power.   *Acts 5:27*
As you sent Christ, now send us.

We pray for those who need healing and hope,
who cannot see the possibility of new life.
As you sent Christ, now send us.

We pray for those in our world who are wounded,
those who suffer from war, oppression, famine, and disease.
As you sent Christ, now send us.

God who is and was and is to be,
be for us the Alpha and Omega,
the beginning and the end, the Almighty.   *Rev. 1:8*
Grant that we might be your forgiveness,
your peace, and your resurrecting good news,
through Jesus Christ, your faithful witness and our Lord,
the firstborn of the dead   *Rev. 1:5*
and the ruler of all the kings of the earth.
Amen.

INVITATION TO THE OFFERING
    God gives new life to all that is,
    including ourselves and all that sustains us.

So let our tithes and offerings
be our songs of praise and thanksgiving   *Ps. 150:1*
in response to the God who loves us and frees us!   *Rev. 1:5*

PRAYER OF THANKSGIVING/DEDICATION
Holy One,
bless our offerings and transform them
into healing for the wounded,
hope for the disheartened,
courage for the frightened,
and faith for the embittered.
In the name of Jesus Christ,
your faithful witness,
the first resurrected, and   *Rev. 1:5*
ruler of the sovereigns of the earth. **Amen.**

CHARGE
Go to celebrate all that God has done   *Ps. 150:2*
as Christ breathes new life into you,   *John 20:22*
sending you out with the Spirit of forgiveness and faith   *John 20:23*
for the life of the world.

BLESSING
May you be filled with the grace and peace of the God
who is and was and is to come,   *Rev. 1:4*
and with the Spirit of Jesus Christ,
God's faithful witness,
who loves us and sets us free.   *Rev. 1:5*

Question for Reflection

Thomas doubted the resurrection until he saw the nail holes and put his
finger in the wound of the risen Christ's hands and side. We, too, have been
wounded in this life, and our society often teaches us to hide our wounds
and vulnerabilities. What might happen if, like Christ, we invited those
shut down by life to explore our wounds?

Household Prayer: Morning

Gracious God,
you are the God
who is and was and is to be.
Thank you that Christ has freed us
to be a kingdom of priests
serving you and your world.
Give me a deeper sense, as I move through this day,
of what it means to say
that you are my "Alpha and Omega," my A to Z. Amen.

Household Prayer: Evening

Jesus, tonight I remember
that your gospel gives me the power to forgive any and all,
through the gift of your Holy Spirit,
and that includes forgiving myself.
Breathe your peace into me
so that even if I pierced you today,
I can still see you coming to embrace me
with your freedom and love this night. Amen

Third Sunday of Easter

Acts 9:1–6 (7–20)   Revelation 5:11–14
Psalm 30   John 21:1–19

OPENING WORDS / CALL TO WORSHIP

O Lord our God, we praise you.   *Ps. 30*
We cried to you for help
and you answered us.
You have restored our lives;
you have rescued us from the grave.

[or]

I looked and heard the voice of angels,   *Rev. 5:11-13*
thousands and thousands around God's throne, singing:
Worthy is the lamb who was slain
to receive power and wealth
and wisdom and might
and honor and glory and blessing!
Then I heard every creature on earth,
and under the earth, and in the sea, singing:
To the one who is seated on the throne
and to the Lamb
be blessing and honor and glory and might
forever and ever!

CALL TO CONFESSION

When your soul is suffering in silence,   *Ps. 30:3*
call out to the Lord our God,
who heals our brokenness,
who lifts us up from the pit
and restores our lives.
Let us confess our sin.

PRAYER OF CONFESSION

Lord God, in the light of your glory
we see the evil we have done,
the suffering we have caused,
the good we have refused,
and the truth we have denied.
Heal us of our sin,
wash us in your mercy,
and feed us with your grace,
so that we may follow your way
and tell the good news of the gospel. Amen.

DECLARATION OF FORGIVENESS

Rise up from the dust!   *Ps. 30:11*
Cast off the shroud of sorrow
and put on the joy of the Lord.
In Jesus Christ we are forgiven.
Thanks be to God.

PRAYER OF THE DAY

Living Lord, you meet us in unexpected places
and surprise us with the abundance of your love.
Feed us by your Word and fill us with your Spirit
so that we may follow you this day, and always;
through Jesus Christ, your Son, our Savior. **Amen.**

PRAYER FOR ILLUMINATION

O God of light,
by the power of your Holy Spirit,
restore our sight,
that in these words of Scripture and sermon
we may see Christ,
in whose name we pray. **Amen.**

PRAYERS OF INTERCESSION

[Possible response to each intercession:]
O Lord our God,   *Ps. 30:2*
we cry to you for help.

We pray for those who are persecuted for
     their faith;   *John 21:19; Acts 9:1*
give them freedom, peace, and safety.

We pray for those who breathe curses and threats;
give them new hearts and new lives to glorify you.

We pray for those who work by day and night;   *John 21:3*
give them satisfaction and rest from their labors.

We pray for those who fear their efforts are in vain;
fill their lives with your providence and grace.

We pray for all who suffer in sickness and grief;   *Ps. 30:11*
give them healing, hope, and joy.

We pray for the faithful in every nation of the earth;   *Rev. 5:11*
give them voices to praise your name forever.

We ask all these things in the name of Jesus,
who loves us, who feeds us, who saves us. **Amen.**

INVITATION TO THE OFFERING
Jesus calls us to feed his lambs   *John 21:15-17*
and tend his sheep.
Let us show and share his love
through the offering of our lives.

PRAYER OF THANKSGIVING/DEDICATION
Worthy are you, O God,   *Rev. 5:12*
to receive power and wealth
and wisdom and might
and honor and glory and blessing.
Receive these gifts
of thanksgiving and praise
and use them for your glory
and the good of your people;
in the name of Jesus Christ, the Lamb. **Amen.**

CHARGE

Jesus said: *John 21:15-17*
Feed my lambs;
tend my sheep.
Follow me.

BLESSING

To the one who is seated on the throne   *Rev. 5:13*
and to the Lamb
be blessing and honor
and glory and might
forever and ever!

Questions for Reflection

Jesus chose Peter, who had denied him in his hour of need, to tend his sheep and build his church. He chose Paul, who had persecuted Jesus' followers, to proclaim the good news of the gospel. Can anything separate us from the love of God in Jesus Christ? What has Jesus chosen and called you to do?

Household Prayer: Morning

Lord Jesus Christ,
as you met your disciples
just after daybreak on the beach,
meet us at the dawning of this new day.
As you filled their nets with fish,
fill our lives with love and grace,
more than we can ask or imagine.
In your holy name we pray. Amen.

Household Prayer: Evening

Gracious God, we praise you
for the blessing of this day
and the promise of tomorrow.
Be our helper as the night falls
and our joy when the morning comes;
through Jesus Christ our Lord. Amen.

Fourth Sunday of Easter

Acts 9:36–43   Revelation 7:9–17
Psalm 23   John 10:22–30

OPENING WORDS / CALL TO WORSHIP

Alleluia, Christ is risen! *Rev. 7:12*
The Lord is risen indeed, Alleluia!
Blessing and honor is yours, O God.
Glory to God forever. Alleluia!

CALL TO CONFESSION

God is present to guide our journey
and eager to forgive us when we go astray;
therefore, in humility and faith,
let us confess our sins against God and neighbor.

PRAYER OF CONFESSION

Holy God, *Ps. 23; Luke 1:79*
we confess that we have strayed
from your paths of right relationship and peace,
and we have dishonored you,
ourselves, and your creation;
we repent of these hurtful ways.
Forgive us, we pray,
as we learn to forgive others,
and guide our feet into the way of peace. Amen.

DECLARATION OF FORGIVENESS

[May be spoken from the font]
God's mercy overflows as a healing spring *Ps. 23; Acts 9:41*
to cleanse us of our offenses;
therefore, know that you are forgiven
and receive new life in Christ.

PRAYER OF THE DAY

Almighty God, to whom all honor belongs,   *Rev. 7:9, 11, 12*
you have gathered a people
from every tribe and language
to praise your name eternally.
Join our song with all of heaven
as we worship you this day
in the glorious light of Christ. **Amen.**

PRAYER FOR ILLUMINATION

Shepherd of Souls,
you call us to an abundant feast
at the table of your word;
open our hearts to feed on your goodness,
that by the power of the Holy Spirit
we might dwell evermore deeply in you. **Amen.**

PRAYERS OF INTERCESSION

In this season of Easter rejoicing,
let us offer our prayers and thanksgivings saying,
O Risen Christ,
Open our eyes to your mercy in the world.

For the goodness of the earth,
that it may flourish with flowing waters,
verdant pastures, and paths that lead us
to protect and care for your creation.
O Risen Christ,
Open our eyes to your mercy in the world.

For the peace and welfare of the world,
that all our tables of work and worship
promote the understanding and dignity
that transform enemies into friends.
O Risen Christ,
Open our eyes to your mercy in the world.

For all who suffer with sickness, need, or danger,
that all our afflictions and fears are met with healing

and the comforting presence of your voice.
O Risen Christ,
Open our eyes to your mercy in the world.

For the blessings we receive and share,
that we may live a life of ceaseless praise
for the salvation that is ours through you.
O Risen Christ,
Open our eyes to your mercy in the world.

For the saints in light,
that you will wipe every tear from their eyes
as they dwell with you eternally.
O Risen Christ,
Open our eyes to your mercy in the world.

Holy God,
you are our hope and our strength,
our light and our sovereign,
our shepherd and our savior.
With all the saints in heaven and on earth,
we praise your holy name
and entrust every care to you;
through Jesus Christ we pray. **Amen.**

INVITATION TO THE OFFERING
"The LORD is my shepherd, I shall not want."   *Ps. 23:1*
Trusting in divine care,
let us present our tithes and offerings to God
who restores our lives eternally.

PRAYER OF THANKSGIVING/DEDICATION
Holy God, Divine Shepherd,
you anoint us with the oil of gladness;
your love overflows our hearts.
Accept our offering for the good of the world
as we joyfully give thanks for our life in you.
In Jesus' name we pray. **Amen.**

CHARGE

> Go forth to follow paths of righteousness; *Ps. 23:3, 6*
> go forth to follow paths of peace;
> and may God's goodness and mercy
> follow you as you serve the risen Lord.

BLESSING

> May Christ the Good Shepherd
> bless and guide you this day and always.

Question for Reflection

Psalm 23 affirms that God supplies our every need. How do our lives change when we trust this great promise of God?

Household Prayer: Morning

Holy God,
you have called a people to be your family
out of every tribe, language, and nation,
to love and serve you daily
in a world of beauty, complexity, and diversity.
Help us to honor and respect
the dignity of difference
as we seek to be one with you and each other
this day and always. Amen.

Household Prayer: Evening

O Shepherd of all,
you have brought us to the close of another day;
for this gift and the blessings we now name,
we give you thanks. . . .
All that we have and all that we are come from you;
and so, trusting in the goodness of your divine care,
let us lie down this night in peace,
that tomorrow we may rise to greet you in resurrection joy. Amen.

Fifth Sunday of Easter

Acts 11:1–18   Revelation 21:1–6
Psalm 148   John 13:31–35

OPENING WORDS / CALL TO WORSHIP
Alleluia! Christ is alive; let all the people praise him.
Let all creation sing with joy. Alleluia!

CALL TO CONFESSION
Trusting in the love of God to make all things new,
let us confess our sin to God and our neighbor.

PRAYER OF CONFESSION
God of mercy, *John: 13:34; Acts 11:9,*
your command to love one another *12, 17, 18*
across all differences
opens us to new horizons,
yet we often respond with fear and judgment
that hinders your goal for humanity.
Forgive our sins, we pray,
and give us a true repentance
that leads to life for all creation.
We pray in Jesus' name. Amen.

DECLARATION OF FORGIVENESS
God's promises are trustworthy and true;
your sins are forgiven.
Be at peace to serve the Lord,
and may you always be known by your love.

PRAYER OF THE DAY

Surprising God, in the resurrection of Jesus Christ   *Rev. 21:5; Acts*
you make all things new.   *11:1–18; John 13:34*
Long ago you called your church
to a love beyond all social and cultural differences
and gave them the gift of your Holy Spirit
to open their hearts to enact such love.
Give us that same spirit of openness,
that we too might discern new directions in our day
for your dream to reconcile and heal all creation.
In Jesus' name we pray. **Amen.**

PRAYER FOR ILLUMINATION

O God of promise,   *Acts 11:16; Rev. 21:5*
your word made flesh in Jesus Christ
is trustworthy and true.
By the power of your Holy Spirit,
may it rise up in us this day like a gift
from the spring of the water of life
to refresh our thirsty souls. **Amen.**

PRAYERS OF INTERCESSION

In this season of Easter rejoicing,
let us offer our prayers and thanksgivings
for the church and the world saying,
O God of love,
Raise us to new life in Christ.

For the well-being of your creation,
that we may promote its ability
to offer praise to you through spacious skies,
bountiful seas, verdant lands,
and precious creatures great and small.
O God of love,
Raise us to new life in Christ.

For the life of the church,
that our generous witness may broaden your table
as all find a place to live and grow in love.

O God of love,
Raise us to new life in Christ.

For the welfare of your world,
that all leaders and people young and old
will strive to live together in harmony
while serving the common good.
O God of love,
Raise us to new life in Christ.

For all who suffer any violence, pain, or grief,
that they will know the comfort of your presence
as you wipe every tear from their eyes.
O God of love,
Raise us to new life in Christ.

For the love made known to us in Jesus Christ
through this community,
for this and all other blessings we give you thanks and praise.
O God of love,
Raise us to new life in Christ.

For all who have died,
that you will bring them to the fullness of your joy,
where mourning and pain will be no more.
O God of love,
Raise us to new life in Christ.

For so many blessings,
and for answered prayers,
we give you thanks through Jesus Christ,
in whose name we pray. **Amen.**

INVITATION TO THE OFFERING

"I give you a new commandment,   *John 13:34*
that you love one another.
Just as I have loved you, you also should love one another."
Let us with gladness offer to God
the gifts of our labor, life, and love.

PRAYER OF THANKSGIVING/DEDICATION

Loving God, we give you thanks
for the ministry of reconciliation to which you call us
in the name of Jesus Christ and his resurrection.
Accept these gifts for your mission to heal all creation.
May they be a testament to your love for us
as we share them in love for you;
through Jesus Christ we pray. **Amen.**

CHARGE

Jesus has loved us so that we may love others. *John 13:34*
Go forth in peace to love and serve the Lord.

BLESSING

May God who has made you a new creation
give you the grace to grow in faith, hope, love, and justice.

Question for Reflection

In Acts 11:1–18, Peter, led by the Spirit, discloses God's new directions
to heal creation, and the church reconfigures its social boundaries. The
Gentiles, who were excluded from the church in Jerusalem because their
eating habits were judged to be vile and unclean, are now included by the
reconciling work of the Spirit. Where is God's Spirit opening us to new
directions in mission this day?

Household Prayer: Morning

Delivering God,
each day we awaken to your goodness
and our hearts cry out in praise
as you set us to tasks for the life of the world.
Do not let us hinder your love,
but strengthen our will,
as we offer thanks in every simple gesture of this day. Amen.

Household Prayer: Evening

Faithful God,
the nightly dance of earth, moon, and stars
speaks of your gift:
love given, love received.
We give thanks this night
for the love you have shown to us this day.
Let us rest in your peace and awaken in joy. Amen.

Sixth Sunday of Easter

Acts 16:9–15   Revelation 21:10; 21:22–22:5
Psalm 67   John 14:23–29 *or* John 5:1–9

OPENING WORDS / CALL TO WORSHIP

Alleluia, Christ is risen.   *Ps. 67:3*
The Lord is risen indeed, alleluia.
Let the peoples praise you, O God.
Let all the peoples praise you.

CALL TO CONFESSION

Do not let your hearts be troubled,   *John 14:27*
but confess your sins and God will give you peace.

PRAYER OF CONFESSION

Loving God,   *John 14:23, 24*
we confess that we are an anxious people
who deny your blessing and fail to keep your word.
Forgive us, we pray, for these and all our sins,
that we might live in peace and reflect your love
in the world;
through Jesus Christ we pray. Amen.

DECLARATION OF FORGIVENESS

Let your hearts be still,
for God loves you and forgives all your wrongdoing.
Beloved, receive the peace of Christ.   *John 14:27*

PRAYER OF THE DAY

Astonishing God,   *Rev. 21:10, 24–26; 22:1–2;*
you give us a vision of the heavenly city,   *Ps. 67; Acts 16:9–15*
the new Jerusalem,

your home among mortals on earth.
All people and nations will stream to your city
where they will find nourishment, healing, and peace.
Even now your blessing shines upon all the earth
to help us see a larger vision
of your loving care for all creation.
And so you call us to move beyond our comfortable circles,
and into unfamiliar places,
as we seek to share your dream
of a world made new in Christ. **Amen.**

PRAYER FOR ILLUMINATION

Living God,   *Acts 16:9–15*
you sent your apostle to preach the gospel
to women gathered by a river,
in a secluded place of prayer.
There a businesswoman named Lydia
was led by the Spirit to hear your word as truth.
You opened her heart in love,
and she opened her home for the spreading of the gospel.
By the power of your Holy Spirit,
fling wide the doors of our hearts this day
as we hear your word of life,
that we too may open our lives to serve your world in love.
In Jesus' name we pray. **Amen.**

PRAYERS OF INTERCESSION

In this season of the Spirit
let us offer our prayers and thanksgivings for the
    world, saying,
Lord, send out your Spirit   *Ps. 103:30*
and renew the face of the earth.

All creation lives to praise you, O God.   *Ps. 67:6*
As the earth yields its blessing,
may we honor and protect the precious gifts of nature
and give thanks for the beauty, healing, and sustenance it
    provides for all.
Lord, send out your Spirit
and renew the face of the earth.

You bless your church throughout all the ages   *Acts 16:9–15*
with leaders like Paul and Lydia
to share in the spreading of the gospel.
Give to your church this day a
profound sense of the mission
to which you now call us
for the life and health of the world.
Lord, send out your Spirit
and renew the face of the earth.

You judge the people with equity   *Ps. 67:4*
and guide the nations of the earth.
Give to all leaders and people
the gift of wisdom and the spirit of peace,
that we may walk by your light as we serve
      the common good.
Lord, send out your Spirit
and renew the face of the earth.

You promise to be with us always   *John 14:25, 26, 28*
through the comfort of your Holy Spirit.
Give to all who suffer violence, grief, or pain
an enduring trust in Jesus that joy will rise again.
Lord, send out your Spirit
and renew the face of the earth.

We give thanks for the many blessings of our lives,   *John 14:25, 26*
that as we follow Jesus,
he journeys with us day by day
through the presence of your Holy Spirit, our Advocate and teacher.
Lord, send out your Spirit
and renew the face of the earth.

You are alpha and omega, the beginning and the end.   *Rev. 22:13*
Be with all who are born this day,
and those who will die,
that your will for them may be fulfilled;
and may we all come to share
in your heavenly city with voices of unending praise.
Amen.

INVITATION TO THE OFFERING

The earth has yielded its increase   *Ps. 67:6*
and God has richly blessed us.
Therefore bring your tithes and offerings
and come into God's courts with praise.

PRAYER OF THANKSGIVING/DEDICATION

Giving God,
as spring bursts forth its blossoms
in witness to your love,
you bless us from generation to generation
with the new life of Easter faith.
All that we have and all that we are come from you, O God,
so we gladly share this offering,
that others too may be blessed,
for the sake of Jesus Christ, in whose name we pray. **Amen.**

CHARGE

Live in love, abide in peace,
and serve the Lord, for God is ever present.

BLESSING

May the Lord be gracious and bless you   *Ps. 67:1, 3*
that you may live a life of praise forever in God's light.

Questions for Reflection

When Lydia hears the gospel, she becomes the first Christian in Europe.
Led by the Spirit, Lydia's faith is decisive and her witness is immediate.
The word opens her heart in love, and she opens her house in hospitality
in service of the gospel. How might Lydia's witness excite your sense of
ministry and mission this day? Where might you find someone searching
for God's word?

Household Prayer: Morning

Holy Spirit,
enliven in us a faith and witness like Lydia's,
that through deepened prayer
we might rise to action in service of the gospel. Amen.

Household Prayer: Evening

God, it is night and the time for rest has come.
We have served you in love this day
and for this we give you thanks.
Do not leave us comfortless,
but send your Spirit to abide with us as we trust in you this night. Amen.

Ascension of the Lord

Acts 1:1–11   Ephesians 1:15–23
Psalm 47 *or* Psalm 93   Luke 24:44–53

OPENING WORDS / CALL TO WORSHIP

The Lord is robed in majesty   *Ps. 93*
and armed with strength.
The Lord has made the world so sure
that it cannot be moved.
The Lord is robed in majesty
and armed with strength.

Ever since the world began,
your throne has been established;
you are from everlasting.
The Lord is robed in majesty
and armed with strength.

Mightier than the sound of many waters,
mightier than the breakers of the sea,
mightier is the Lord
who dwells on high.
The Lord is robed in majesty
and armed with strength.

Your testimonies are very sure,
and holiness befits your house,
O Lord, forever and forever more.
The Lord is robed in majesty
and armed with strength.

CALL TO CONFESSION

Let us come before God with contrite hearts,
acknowledging our sin and trusting in forgiveness.

PRAYER OF CONFESSION

[A time of silence may be kept.]
Merciful God,
day by day we have failed to believe
in your presence and your promised forgiveness.
We have not trusted in your power
to give the riches we cannot see.
We have not honored our sisters and brothers
as heirs of your desired peace.
We have not forgiven others or ourselves.
Give us the wisdom and faith to be your body on earth,
that we may rejoice in the presence of your saving bounty,
to the glory of your ascended Son. Amen.

DECLARATION OF FORGIVENESS

By the power of the Holy Spirit,
as a witness to the death and resurrection of Christ Jesus
and the assurance of pardon in Jesus' name,
I proclaim to you the forgiveness of all your sins,
that with renewed life you may
serve this creation and the people of God
in peace and strength.
God is with you.

PRAYER OF THE DAY

Holy God of every time and every place,
you gather us to hear of Jesus.
Help us see your infinite life
in our own community and in all of creation,
we pray in your holy name. **Amen.**

PRAYER FOR ILLUMINATION

By the power of the Holy Spirit
open our minds to the Word, your Son,
who comes to us as one of us and
ascends to the heavens to remain with us. **Amen.**

PRAYERS OF INTERCESSION

Let us pray for the church, the world, and all who are in need, saying,
Hear us, O God; your mercy is great.

We give you thanks for the community of faith throughout the world.
According to your compassion, Holy God,
guide your church to proclaim the gospel
so that its wide-open door is apparent to everyone;
heal the great chasms that exist between our peoples;
help our leaders and teachers to shepherd us with wisdom.
Hear us, O God; **your mercy is great.**

We give you thanks for nations and leaders.
By your power, O God, inspire all people
to insist on just economies and social structures;
prepare our young people to turn their zeal into peace;
unbind those who are discouraged,
and teach us all to persevere.
Hear us, O God; **your mercy is great.**

We give you thanks for all creation.
Open our eyes and ears
to see and know more about this earthly home,
which you created for your joy and ours.
Show us how to love the creatures and plants
we would otherwise ignore and neglect.
Hear us, O God; **your mercy is great.**

Merciful Lord,
we pray for those among your people here and throughout the world
who are in trouble—
the sick and hungry,
those who are unjustly imprisoned and abused,
children without shelter,
adults without work.
Hear us, O God; **your mercy is great.**

Hear now the prayers of your people spoken silently or aloud . . . .
(*A time of silence is kept.*)
Hear us, O God; **your mercy is great.**

We give you thanks for the saints
whose witness has nourished our faith throughout the ages,
    especially N.
Their assurance in word and deed has fed us with the truth of
    your Word,
      Hear us, O God; **your mercy is great.**

Ascended Lord,
we trust that you will hear our prayers
and answer with what we need.
We pray this in the name of the Father, Son, and Holy Spirit,
One God, Mother of us all. **Amen.**

INVITATION TO THE OFFERING

For the gifts of Jesus' life, death, resurrection, and ascension,
and for the privilege of offering the fruits of our hands,
let us give thanks to God with what we have this day.

PRAYER OF THANKSGIVING/DEDICATION

Gracious and giving God,
you are the One who first has given to us
all that we need for life.
Guide us to use what we now gather
for the well-being of your church,
for those in need of shelter and food,
for all who suffer for want of your Word,
and for nurturing faith in your people.
In the name of Christ Jesus, our Lord. **Amen.**

CHARGE

Go forth with the spirit
of wisdom and hope,
with eyes enlightened
and minds aroused by the power of Christ.
Be assured that wherever you go,
Christ is with you.
Be kind to all who are sent your way
because of the Holy Spirit
who gives you the power.

BLESSING

Now may the One who gives you all that you are,
strengthen you in faith and hope,
this day and forevermore.

Question for Reflection

How is your faith strengthened by knowing that we do not look for Jesus
in only one place but find the Risen One everywhere, because he has
ascended to the throne of God?

Household Prayer: Morning

Gracious God,
we thank you for bringing us through the night
and for making this new day.
You send us out rested and uplifted by your presence.
Wherever we go,
whatever our work today,
whomever we meet,
help us to greet our tasks and our leisure with joy.
We give you thanks, through Jesus, our Lord. Amen.

Household Prayer: Evening

Wondrous Lord,
we marvel that this day has ended,
filled with marks of your love even in moments of strife.
Now give us rest.
Comfort those who have no bed this night,
and keep them safe.
We bow our heads in gratitude
for food, work, friends, family, challenges, and accomplishments.
We pray this in the name of the One
who watches over us day and night. Amen.

Seventh Sunday of Easter

Acts 16:16–34   Revelation 22:12–14, 16–17, 20–21
Psalm 97   John 17:20–26

OPENING WORDS / CALL TO WORSHIP

The Spirit and the bride say, "Come."   *Rev. 22:13, 17*
Let everyone who is thirsty come.
Let everyone who hears say, "Come."
Let everyone who is thirsty come.
Let anyone who wishes take the water of life as a gift.
Let everyone who is thirsty come.
Come to the tree of life, the Alpha and the Omega.
Amen. Come, Lord Jesus.

CALL TO CONFESSION

Trusting in the promise of grace,
let us tell the whole truth about ourselves
and beg God's mercy
for the renewal and amendment of our lives.

PRAYER OF CONFESSION

Gracious Power,
you call us to your everlasting springs
to be drenched and reformed,
but we fail to heed you.
We do not turn with love to our neighbors
to ourselves, or to you.
Forgive us for our failings,
shield us from our due,
and guide us into unity with all
for the sake of the whole world. Amen.

DECLARATION OF FORGIVENESS

In the compassion of the God who prays for us,
with us, and in us,
you are forgiven,
for the sake of the one who was sent
to show us the face of love
and who died and rose,
one with the Father and with us.

PRAYER OF THE DAY

O God, who opens our prison doors and releases us from our faults,
keep us near to you in the hours of each day
that by the power of the prayer Jesus prays for us
and the light of your Word
we might drink of your living water, know true joy,
and serve you to the end of time. **Amen.**

PRAYER FOR ILLUMINATION

Holy God,
whose voice is heard in the thunder and in the silence,
speak to us now,
by the power of your Spirit,
that we may hear your word for us today.
In Jesus' name we ask it. **Amen.**

PRAYERS OF INTERCESSION

Our Lord Jesus prayed for us that we might be one.
Let us pray as one for the needs of the world, for the church,
and for all with whom Jesus desires our unity, saying,
Holy God, hear our prayer.

God, our lifeblood and our light,
you show us your new creation every day.
You feed and clothe us and give us joy in your good earth.
We praise you—our home and our true blessing.
Holy God, **hear our prayer.**

For unity among all peoples—
the body of Christ, rent by conflict, that we may be one;

for people of all faiths to honor one another;
and for the end to religious wars.
  Holy God, **hear our prayer.**

For peace among nations, between tribes,
on school yards, in academic halls,
within legislative bodies, and around kitchen tables in every home.
  Holy God, **hear our prayer.**

For the church's mission to proclaim the good news,
that the world might know you;
may the new life possible in faith
break open all people to love one another.
  Holy God, **hear our prayer.**

For the well-being of the earth and its creatures;
for the oceans and rivers, heavens and depths, soil and dust;
for plants and fish and birds and mammals,
who together with ourselves are fed and blessed each day
by the air, food, and water you provide.
  Holy God, **hear our prayer.**

For all people who cry out to you in this hardened time;
for people who do not have work, those who have no safety net;
those without dining tables or beds;
those who do not have enough food.
  Holy God, **hear our prayer.**

For those concerns we name now silently or aloud . . .
[A time of silence is kept.]
  Holy God, **hear our prayer.**

For the saints of all times and places,
by whose faith and hope we have been nurtured
in accord with Jesus' prayer for his people
and our prayers for each other.
  Holy God, **hear our prayer.**

Into your hands, Gracious God,
we pray all these things,

asking you to hear our thanksgivings and our pleas,
knowing you hear more than we can say
and will grant what is needed; in Jesus' name. **Amen.**

INVITATION TO THE OFFERING

Give now with generous hearts
that all people may hear God's Word
and be helped by the work of this church.

PRAYER OF THANKSGIVING/DEDICATION

Eternal God,
who brings joy out of sorrow,
plenty out of want,
life out of death:
we thank you for the treasures of the earth,
your creation, filled with your blessing,
for it was in company with these earthly things
that your Son came to dwell,
showing us the enormity of your love.
Because of Jesus' resurrection from the dead,
we, too, are brought to new life,
called to pray and work for the renewal of others.
Take these offerings for the sake of the one without whom
our poverty would be extreme,
Jesus Christ our Lord. **Amen.**

CHARGE

Your chains are broken;
your prison doors are open.
Go forth, then, with joy
to live as one
with the God who sends you out.
Let the hope that is in you,
free you daily
that through you,
the Holy Spirit may free others.

BLESSING

Now may the power that is in Christ Jesus,
the strength of the Holy Spirit to baptize and save,

and the fierce love of God, the Creator,
keep you in grace and truth.

Questions for Reflection

What chains bind you or the people of your community at this time in
your life? Where each day do you notice the freedom of Christ working to
break the chains apart?

Household Prayer: Morning

Good and gracious God,
we rise with the morning light
to give you thanks for rest and dreams,
for warmth and safety,
for the delight we have again today
in a life filled with your goodness.
Keep us in your care this day
that we may walk in your path,
glad for our friends,
praying for our enemies,
and eager to hear your Word;
in Jesus' name. Amen.

Household Prayer: Evening

Merciful God,
for all that we have done and failed to do this day
we turn to you for respite.
Forgive us for having shunned your desires;
rejoice with us over moments that have filled us with joy.
Bless your people in every land with peace.
Protect us now through the night
that we may wake again to praise your name.
Let the Holy Spirit abide in this house. Amen.

Day of Pentecost

Acts 2:1–21 *or* Genesis 11:1–9   Romans 8:14–17 *or* Acts 2:1–21
Psalm 104:24–34, 35b   John 14:8–17 (25–27)

OPENING WORDS / CALL TO WORSHIP

How manifold are your works, O Lord!   *Ps. 104:24, 30, 33*
In wisdom you have made them all;
the earth is full of your creatures.

You send forth your spirit,
and they are created;
and so you renew
the face of the earth.

I will sing to the Lord as long as I live;
I will praise my God
while I have my being.

CALL TO CONFESSION

Our sister Julian of Norwich spoke these words of faith:
"All people who shall be saved, while we are in this world,
have in us a marvellous mixture of both weal [well-being] and woe.
We have in us our risen Lord Jesus;
we have in us the misery of the harm of Adam's falling and dying.
We are steadfastly protected by Christ,
and by the touch of his grace we are raised into sure trust of salvation.
And by Adam's fall our perceptions are so shattered in various ways,
by sins and by different sufferings,
that we are so darkened and blinded that we can hardly find any
    comfort."*
In the strong assurance of pardon, let us confess our sin.

*Julian of Norwich, *Revelations of Divine Love*, trans. Elizabeth Spearing (New York: Penguin
Books, 1998), 125.

181

PRAYER OF CONFESSION

Without your power, O God, we are lost.
We have done the things we would avoid,
and what you desire, we have not done.
By your purifying fire transform our lives;
guide us into honesty and compassion
so that filled with your peace
our dreams and visions may be one with yours;
through Jesus Christ, our Savior and Lord. Amen.

DECLARATION OF FORGIVENESS

Everyone who calls on the name of the Lord shall
    be saved. *Acts 2:21*
By the power in whom we live and move and have
    our being,
I pronounce to you the complete forgiveness of all
    your sins,
through the holy Trinity, one God,
whose mercy is everlasting. **Amen.**

PRAYER OF THE DAY

Holy God, who comes to us in breath,
visits us from the throne of heaven,
and sets us aflame with amazement and joy,
you open our paths to new visions
and guide our feet deeper into your wisdom.
Give us faith to trust your presence,
through Jesus Christ, who lives and reigns with you
and the Holy Spirit, one God, now and forever. **Amen.**

PRAYER FOR ILLUMINATION

Holy Wisdom, you are the pillar of fire
that leads us into each new moment of our lives.
By the power of your Spirit,
settle now into our hearts and illumine your will;
through Jesus Christ, our Lord. **Amen.**

PRAYERS OF INTERCESSION

With joy for the gift of the Holy Spirit,
together, let us pray for the well-being of the church,
the world, and all in need, saying,
God, in your mercy, hear our prayer.

We thank you for the wonder that erupted on the day
    of Pentecost,
for the birth of the church,
for the gifts of amazement and challenge,
and for all the witnesses whose lives have been altered
by your power alive in our world.
    God, in your mercy, **hear our prayer.**

For the many peoples of this earth
whose visions differ,
whose languages offer special insights,
whose ways of worship and compassion feed our own,
we thank you.
    God, in your mercy, **hear our prayer.**

For the earth itself,
through whose creatures we see your love
and in whose winds we remember the coming of the Spirit,
we thank you.
    God, in your mercy, **hear our prayer.**

Make us grateful for the confounding experiences
the Holy Spirit's presence creates in our lives,
for the marvel of new visions,
for the wisdom in prophetic words,
and for the prayers of your great high priest.
    God, in your mercy, **hear our prayer.**

Make us hungry to protect the health and nurturance
    of all people;
let your fire burn in the leaders of the nations,
in governors and mayors,
on city councils and school boards;

guard the lives of peacemakers, soldiers, philosophers,
    and artists.
Pool the skills and passion of all your people
for the sake of our delight and the nourishment of others.
    God, in your mercy, **hear our prayer.**

Give comfort to all people who are refugees from war
    and famine,
those who are lonely and frightened,
ill, imprisoned, homeless, or without work,
and those who face death today.
We pray especially for those we name now silently or aloud . . .
[A time of silence is kept.]
    God, in your mercy, **hear our prayer.**

Knowing it is your Holy Spirit
who has flowed through your witnesses of ages past,
we give you thanks for all the saints who have gone before us,
especially *N.*
With them, and with confidence that you hear our prayers,
we commend all for whom we lift our voices,
trusting that you give more than we need.
Through your Son, Jesus Christ, our Lord. **Amen.**

INVITATION TO THE OFFERING
Because God first loved us,
we are made to love one another.
For the sake of the life of the world, offer yourselves,
your time, and your possessions as signs of love.

PRAYER OF DEDICATION
Make us thankful every day, O God,
for the gifts that alight upon us from your bounty.
Guide us to use these offerings to your glory
for the health of your people and this creation. **Amen.**

CHARGE

Love the commandments,
keep them, honor them,
do right by your neighbors,
and listen to the Spirit.

BLESSING

Now may the Advocate, the Holy Spirit,
guide you in the ways of God
and fill you with the peace that only Christ can give.

Questions for Reflection

What gift of yours, of your family, and of your community has the Holy
Spirit especially nurtured in recent times? How might that gift be expressed
and used in a new way in the coming year?

Household Prayer: Morning

Gracious God,
we thank you for the peace of good sleep
and for keeping us safe throughout the night.
Let this new day be a time of praise and joy
as we go out to meet you in our sisters and brothers.
We pray this in Jesus' name. Amen.

Household Prayer: Evening

Merciful Lord, as night comes to this house,
we thank you for the challenges and accomplishments of this day.
Give our hearts and minds the comfort now to rest in your care,
trusting that whatever tomorrow brings,
your hand will be ready to catch us if we fall. Amen.

❧ ADDITIONAL RESOURCES ❧

Greetings

[It is appropriate to begin each service with a greeting quoted or drawn from Scripture. You may choose to use the same greeting for several weeks or throughout a season.]

Grace and peace in Jesus Christ our Lord.   *Ps. 27:1*
Amen.
The Lord is our light and our salvation
Thanks be to God.

Grace to you and peace from God our Father   *2 Thess. 1:2*
and the Lord Jesus Christ.

Grace and peace from the One God
who comes to us as
Lover, the Beloved, and Love itself.

The grace of our Lord Jesus Christ,
the love of God,
and the communion of the Holy Spirit
be with you all.
And also with you.

Blessed be the triune God
who created all things,
who renews and sustains us,
who pours out upon us
the fullness of peace.
Amen.

The grace and mercy of the Blessed Trinity,
One God,
maker, redeemer, and sustainer of all things,
be with you all.
And also with you.

Thanksgiving for Baptism I

Blessed is your name, O God,
   and gracious is your constancy.
Over the waters, your Spirit brooded,
   and you formed land and sea, sun and moon,
   animals, birds, plants, and humans.
You nourish the fields,
   feed the oceans,
   and blanket the mountains with water and snow.
You make your rain fall on the just and the unjust,
   and fill the air with fog and mist.
We give you thanks for water.

Through waters you made a path for your people.
You saved Noah's family, and creatures two-by-two, from the flood.
You led Pharaoh's daughter to pull Moses from the river.
Parting the waters,
   you saved your people from slavery.
Crossing the waters into the promised land,
   your people found a home.
Flowing out of a rock in the desert,
   water delivered your people from death.
We give you thanks for water.

In the River Jordan, John baptized Jesus of Nazareth,
   who proclaimed a new Reign of God and
   forgiveness from sin.
Beside the well, Jesus asked the woman of Samaria for a drink.
   He gave her healing water and new life.

Through his death, resurrection, and ascension,
    he sends us out: "Go into all the lands, baptizing."
Because your saints in every age have washed your servants
    for life abundant in your triune name,
we give you thanks for water.

Living water, river of life, font of hope, receive our praise
for wind and rain,
for creatures and trees,
for hot and cold,
for the life-blood of Earth,
and for our yearning
    that this home you have made will thrive in your care:
    your waters whole and clean,
    blue and green, growing what is needed,
    immersing us for lives of thanksgiving,
in the name of the one who lives and reigns with you and the Holy Spirit,
one God, now and forever. **Amen.**

Thanksgiving for Baptism II

Holy Creator of all that exists,
blessed be your name throughout the ages.
Before the beginning of time
you separated waters from waters
making Earth and all stars.
 To the dry land, you give rainfall and mist.
 To the seas, you give deeps and currents.
 To the creatures and plants, you give the water of life.
Praise to you for water.

Your Spirit churned over the waters
and into the hearts of your people,
rescuing us from floods and legions.
 To the thirsty, you give a drink of cold water.
 Into the repentant, you pour the cup of salvation.
 For the destitute, you offer a pool of healing.
Praise to you for water.

Through the baptism of your Son,
by his body washed in the waters of the Jordan River,
you baptized the waters of all the Earth.
 We bathe in water blessed by Jesus.
 We drink the water blessed by Jesus.
The water of your creation frees us,
 teaches us, and binds us to you.
Praise to you for water.

Make us grateful for the gifts of healing water,
  beautiful water,
  flowing water,
  nourishing water.
Make us thirsty, O God, for your living water,
in the name of the one by whose water and blood,
we live and move and have our being,
one God, now and forever. **Amen.**

Great Prayers of Thanksgiving / Eucharistic Prayers

[These prayers are offered as supplementary resources that are intended to be in line with approved and published denominational worship materials. They may be adapted for your congregational context.]

FOR GENERAL USE

The Lord be with you.
And also with you.
Lift up your hearts.
We lift them to the Lord.
Let us give thanks to the Lord our God.
It is right to give our thanks and praise.
Holy God, we praise you for your love:
bringing order out of chaos,
breathing life into dust,
leading captives into freedom,
consuming false idols with holy fire,
calling wandering children home,
giving bread to the hungry,
   giving drink to the thirsty,
   raising the dead to life.
Therefore we join our voices with saints and angels
and all the faithful of every time and place, singing,

Holy, holy, holy Lord, God of power and might,
heaven and earth are full of your glory.
Hosanna in the highest.

**Blessed is he who comes in the name of the Lord.
Hosanna in the highest.**

We give you thanks for Jesus Christ:
Word made flesh,
light of the world,
   living water,
      shepherd and gate,
         way and truth and life.
[touching bread]
We give you thanks that the Lord Jesus
on the night before he died, took bread,
and after giving thanks to you, he broke it,
and gave it to his disciples, saying,
Take, eat. This is my body, given for you.
Do this in remembrance of me.
[touching cup]
In the same way Jesus took the cup, saying,
This cup is the new covenant sealed in my blood,
shed for you for the forgiveness of sins.
Whenever you drink it,
do this in remembrance of me.
Remembering your gracious acts,
we offer our lives to you in service and praise
as we keep the feast that Christ prepares:
[lifting bread] bread of heaven,
[lifting cup] cup of salvation,
[lifting bread and cup] resurrection and life.
Great is the mystery of faith:
**Christ has died,
Christ is risen,
Christ will come again.**

Gracious God,
now pour out your Holy Spirit among us:
in this bread,
in this cup,
in your people;
one in the body,

one in the blood,
one with Christ,
one in mission,
one in ministry;
in this place,
in every place,
in this world,
in the world to come.
Through Christ, with Christ, in Christ,
in the unity of the Holy Spirit,
all glory and honor are yours,
almighty God, now and forever. **Amen.**

ADVENT

The Lord be with you.
And also with you.
Lift up your hearts.
We lift them to the Lord.
Let us give thanks to the Lord our God.
It is right to give our thanks and praise.

How can we thank you, O God?
For sun and moon and stars,
for breath and life and all things good,
for your steadfast promise and your faithful love,
for the day that is surely coming
when all things will be made new.

With saints, with angels, and with the whole creation,
we join the ancient and eternal hymn:

Holy, holy, holy Lord, God of power and might,
heaven and earth are full of your glory.
Hosanna in the highest.
Blessed is he who comes in the name of the Lord.
Hosanna in the highest.

We give you thanks, Holy God, for Jesus,
who came to be your living Word,
to baptize us with Spirit and fire,
to feed the hungry, to humble the mighty,
and to announce the good news of your coming realm.

With thanksgiving, we remember how, when the hour had come,
Jesus took his place at the table with the apostles.

He said to them, I will not eat this Passover again
until it is fulfilled in the kingdom of God.

Then Jesus took bread,
and when he had given thanks,
he broke it and gave it to them, saying,
This is my body, which is given for you.
Do this in remembrance of me.

After supper, he took a cup, saying,
This cup that is poured out for you
is the new covenant in my blood.
I will not drink of the fruit of the vine
until the kingdom of God comes.

With thanks and praise we offer ourselves to you,
sharing this holy meal,
remembering Christ's dying and rising,
and praying: Come Lord Jesus!

Christ has died,
Christ is risen,
Christ will come again.

Pour out your Holy Spirit upon us—
this bread, this cup, these people—
Christ's body and blood,
given in love for the world.
Make us one in the Spirit,
one in the church,
and one with Christ our Lord.

Make us gentle, joyful, thankful people,
serving our neighbors, worshiping you alone.
Keep us in the peace of Christ
until you gather us at your table in glory.

Even now, a voice is crying in the wilderness:
prepare the way of the Lord!

Through Christ, with Christ, in Christ,
in the unity of the Holy Spirit,
all glory and honor are yours, almighty God,
now and forever. **Amen.**

CHRISTMAS DAY

The Lord be with you.
And also with you.
Lift up your hearts.
We lift them to the Lord.
Let us give our thanks to the Lord our God.
It is right to give our thanks and praise.

It is good to give you thanks,
O God, source of abundant life;
through Jesus Christ your eternal Word
who creates all things
by the working of your Spirit.

For he is the reflection of your glory,   *Heb. 1:3*
the very imprint of your being.
In him you have become one with us
that we might become one with you.

And so we raise our voices with saints and angels
and all creation in joyful praise to you singing,

Holy, holy, holy Lord, God of goodness and life,
heaven and earth are full of your glory.
Hosanna in the highest.
Blessed is the one who comes in the name of the Lord.
Hosanna in the highest.

Holy and wondrous God,
long ago you spoke to our ancestors
in many and various ways.
And in these last days you have spoken to us
in your Word made flesh, Jesus,
who proclaimed your dream of peace.

Heb. 1:1–2

He gave himself for our weary world,
accepting death so that we might live,
and held our darkness deep within
until through cross and grave and empty tomb
he set us free for love.

On the night before he died for us
our Lord Jesus Christ took bread,
and when he had given thanks to you,
he broke it, and gave it to his disciples, and said,

Take, eat. This is my body, which is given for you.
Do this for the remembrance of me.
After supper he took the cup of wine;
and when he had given thanks,
he gave it to them and said,
Drink this all of you.
This is my blood poured out for you and for all
for the forgiveness of sins.
Whenever you drink it,
do this for the remembrance of me.

And so we proclaim the mystery of faith:
Christ has died,
Christ is risen,
Christ will come again.

Recalling his death and resurrection,
and longing for his coming in glory
we offer you these gifts of bread and wine,
and our lives in thanks and praise.

Pour out your Spirit upon these gifts that they may be for us
the body and blood of our Savior Jesus Christ.
Pour out your Spirit upon us that we might be
a people of grace and truth,
bearing good news of joy in every season.

And bring us at the last with [Mary and Joseph, and] all your saints
to that vision of eternal splendor for which you have created us.
Through Jesus Christ our Lord,
by him, with him, and in him,
in the unity of the Holy Spirit,
we worship you, O God,
in songs of everlasting praise. **Amen.**

EPIPHANY

[The words of institution may be spoken at the breaking of the bread.]

The Lord be with you.
And also with you.
Lift up your hearts.
We lift them up to the lord.
Let us give thanks to the Lord our God.
It is right to give our thanks and praise.

It is right and our joy,
Creator God,
to give you thanks and praise.
For in the beginning you created
the heavens and the earth.
Out of darkness and chaos,
you brought light and order.
You have given life to every living thing
and made us in your image, male and female.
Even when we turned away from you,
loving darkness rather than light,
you did not turn away from us.
You sent prophets to show us the way.

In the fullness of time,
you sent your Son to be Immanuel,
God with us.
At his birth,
the night sky lit up

with heavenly host and a guiding star.
Shepherds and magi found their way to you.
Women and children, tax collectors and lepers
continued to find their way to you.
The darkness of Gethsemane, the cross,
and the grave could not overcome you;
for you are the light of the world,
shining still.

Gracious God,
pour out your Holy Spirit
upon these gifts of bread and wine,
that the bread we break and the cup we bless
may be the communion of the body and blood of Christ.
In this feast, make us one with you
and with each other.
Enflame us with your Spirit,
that we may be united in ministry in every place.
Send us, in your marvelous light,
into the world, ready to serve others and work for peace.
We pray in the triune name of God. **Amen.**

PALM SUNDAY / PASSION SUNDAY

[The words of institution may be spoken at the breaking of the bread.]

The Lord be with you.
And also with you.
Lift up your hearts.
We lift them up to the Lord.
Let us give thanks to the Lord our God.
It is right to give our thanks and praise.

Holy God,
you created the heavens and the earth,
sea and dry ground, creeping things and flying birds,
mountains and plains, desert sands and forest canopies.
All around us, the beauty of your handiwork is evident.
We praise you for such wonder!
In love and freedom, you gave us your blessing
to eat from every plant and from the fruit of the trees.
In return for your generosity and abundance,
we grasped for more than you gave us,
separating ourselves from you through sin.

Yet even when we were unfaithful,
you remained faithful to us.
You continued to give us the gift of your good creation.
When we were bound as slaves,
you gave us freedom by opening a pathway through the sea.
When we complained in the desert,
you gave us water to drink and manna to eat.

When we wandered from your ways,
you sent prophets to call us back and give us hope.
As Isaiah promised, we went out in joy and were led back in peace.
It seemed to us that the mountains and hills burst into song,
and the trees of the field clapped their hands
in praise of your power and faithfulness.

Then, in the fullness of time,
you sent your Son to save us.
Jesus preached and healed;
he taught and challenged us;
he loved and encouraged us.
Yet our songs of praise became shouts of death.
Palm branches lifted high in honor were left in the dust.
At the cross, when we had turned away,
he offered forgiveness and eternal life.
We thank you for such wondrous love as this.

Gracious God,
pour out your Holy Spirit upon us
and upon these gifts of bread and wine.
As Christ broke bread in that upper room
and shared the cup with his disciples,
so may this meal be our communion
in the body and blood of Christ.
By your Spirit, unite us with him
and with all who are baptized in his name,
so that we may offer our own Hosanna
to the one who has come and is coming again.
Strengthen us in the days of the holy week before us,
and for all the days to our life's end,
to recognize this one who comes humbly
and so to follow him.
We pray in the name of Jesus Christ, crucified, risen, and coming again.
Amen.

HOLY THURSDAY

The Lord be with you.
And also with you.
Lift up your hearts.
We lift them to the Lord.
Let us give thanks to the Lord our God.
It is right to give our thanks and praise.

We love you, Lord, for you have heard our cry.   *Ps. 116:1*

When we were captives, enslaved to sin,
you led us safely through the sea
so that we might worship you in freedom.   *Exod. 12:1–14*

Therefore we offer this sacrifice of thanksgiving
and call upon your holy name: *Ps. 116:17*

Holy, holy, holy Lord, God of power and might,
heaven and earth are full of your glory.
Hosanna in the highest.
Blessed is he who comes in the name of the Lord.
Hosanna in the highest.

You are holy, O God of majesty,
and blessed is Jesus Christ our Lord.

He came from you, he returned to you;
you put all things in his hands.   *John 13:3*

He came to show your great love for the world,
and he loved us to the end.   *John 13:1*

With thanksgiving, we remember that the Lord Jesus
on the night when he was betrayed took a loaf of bread,
and when he had given thanks, he broke it and said,
This is my body that is given for you.
Do this in remembrance of me.

In the same way he took the cup after supper, saying,
This cup is the new covenant in my blood.
Do this, as often as you drink it, in remembrance of me.   *1 Cor. 11:23–26*

According to his commandment:
We remember his death,
we proclaim his resurrection,
we await his coming in glory.

Pour out your Holy Spirit upon us
and upon these your gifts of bread and wine,
that the bread we break and the cup we bless
may be the communion of the body and blood of Christ.
By your Spirit make us one with Christ and one another,
that we may serve one another with humility and grace,
following Christ's example, washing one another's feet.   *John 13:14*

Through Christ, with Christ, in Christ,
in the unity of the Holy Spirit,
all glory and honor are yours, almighty God,
now and forever. **Amen.**

EASTER

The Lord be with you.
And also with you.
Lift up your hearts.
We lift them to the Lord.
Let us give thanks to the Lord our God.
It is right to give our thanks and praise.

This is the day that you have made, O Lord—
the first day of the week,
when you created light out of darkness
by the power of your Word and Spirit,
when you created life out of death,
raising Jesus from the grave.

On this first day of the week
we await the coming of your new creation,
when we will be glad and rejoice forever,
    singing,   *Ps. 118:24; Isa. 65:17–18*

Holy, holy, holy Lord, God of power and might,
heaven and earth are full of your glory.
Hosanna in the highest.
Blessed is he who comes in the name of the Lord.
Hosanna in the highest.

You are holy, O God of majesty,
and blessed is Jesus Christ our Lord.

With thanksgiving, we remember his words:
I have eagerly desired to eat this Passover with you. *Luke 22:15*

We remember how he took a loaf of bread,
and when he had given thanks, he broke it
and gave it to his disciples, saying,
This is my body, which is given for you.
Do this in remembrance of me.

We remember how he took the cup after supper, saying,
This cup that is poured out for you
is the new covenant in my blood. *Luke 22: 20*
Whenever you drink it, remember me.

As death came through Adam,
resurrection has come through Christ.

Christ our Lord is coming again to reign
and to put all enemies under his feet. *1 Cor. 15:21, 25*

Praise to you, Lord Jesus:
Dying you destroyed our death,
rising you restored our life.
Lord Jesus, come in glory.

God of grace, pour out your Holy Spirit upon us
and upon these your gifts of bread and wine.

Make us one people, one body in Christ,
as we seek to show your steadfast love
and proclaim the good news of salvation. *Ps. 118:1–2, 14*

Make a place for us at your heavenly banquet
so that we may eat and drink with thanksgiving
when all things are fulfilled in your holy realm. *Luke 22:16*

Through Christ, with Christ, in Christ,
in the unity of the Holy Spirit,

all glory and honor are yours, almighty God,
now and forever. **Amen.**

[*At the breaking of the bread*]
And he was known to them
in the breaking of the bread.   *Luke 24:35*

PENTECOST

The Lord be with you.
And also with you.
Lift up your hearts.
We lift them to the Lord.
Let us give thanks to the Lord our God.
It is right to give our thanks and praise.

O Lord our God, how great are your works.
You created the world and all that is in it.   *Ps. 104:24*
You give the nations their names . . .
*[People in the congregation may be invited to name the nations
and places from which they come.]*

We rebelled against your sovereign love,
seeking to storm the gates of heaven,
trying to make a name for ourselves in the world.   *Gen. 11:1–9*

But by the grace of our Lord Jesus Christ
you have given us your own name
and have made us your own people,
a royal priesthood, a holy nation.   *1 Pet. 2:9–10*

Now send forth your life-giving Spirit
to renew and re-create us.   *Ps. 104:30*
Save us, Lord! We call upon your name: *Acts 2:21*

[During the Sanctus ("Holy, holy, holy") persons in the congregation may sing, shout, or whisper "holy" in a variety of languages.]

Holy, holy, holy Lord, God of power and might,
heaven and earth are full of your glory.
Hosanna in the highest.
Blessed is he who comes in the name of the Lord.
Hosanna in the highest.

Lord God, we have seen your glory
in the face of Jesus Christ. *John 14:9, 2 Cor. 4:6*

We give you thanks
that you have made us one with him
as he is one with you and the Holy Spirit. *John 14:8–17*

By the gift of your Spirit, you have promised
to fulfill the prayers that we ask in Jesus' name. *John 14:14*

By the grace of your Spirit, we have promised
to live in Christ's love and keep his commandments. *John 14:15*

With thanksgiving, we remember
how Jesus took bread, blessed and broke it,
and gave it to his disciples, saying,
This is my body, given for you.

With thanksgiving, we remember
how Jesus took the cup, saying,
This is the new covenant in my blood.
Do this, remembering me. *Luke 22:14–20*

When Jesus ascended into heaven
you sent your Holy Spirit
to teach us, guide us,
and abide in us forever. *John 14:16–17, 25–27*

Remembering your mighty acts of mercy,
we celebrate this feast with the risen Lord,
offering our lives in thanksgiving and praise.

Great is the mystery of faith:
Christ has died,
Christ is risen,
Christ will come again.

Fill this place with your Holy Spirit
like the rush of a mighty wind,
like a consuming fire.   *Acts 2:1–3*

By the power of your Spirit
feed us with bread from heaven
and fill us with the new wine of your reign.   *John 6:51; Acts 2:13*

Make us your sons and daughters,
faithful, fearless, and free.   *Rom. 8:14–17*

Teach us to proclaim
the good news of salvation
to all the nations of the world.   *Acts 2:11*

Fill us with dreams and visions
of that great and glorious day
when the Lord Jesus Christ will come again,
and we will eat and drink with him
in the joy of your eternal realm.   *Acts 2:17–21; Luke 22:14–18*

Through Christ, with Christ, in Christ,
in the unity of the Holy Spirit,
all glory and honor are yours, Almighty God,
now and forever. **Amen.**

Scripture Index